The Wild West Show
A Tangle of Tales and Titles

Occasional Papers in Folklore
No. 4

Ed Cray,[1]
Richard Reuss[2] and
John Patrick[3]

The Wild West Show
A Tangle of Tales and Titles

How Ben Jonson's "Humours of Bartholomew Fair" Became "The Wild West Show," A Contemporary Rugby and Very Bawdy Song

Cray, Ed, Richard Reuss, and John Patrick. The Wild West Show: A Tangle of Tales and Titles. St. Paul: Loomis House, 2014. Print.

© 2014 by Ed Cray

CAMSCO Music
www.camscomusic.com

Loomis House Press
www.loomishousepress.com

ISBN 978-1-935243-95-3

Cover illustration: Detail from the frontispiece of *Sergeant Bell and His Raree-Show*, 1839.

For Fran,
who followed Van Amberg wherever he led

ACKNOWLEDGEMENTS

A number of people have contributed material, comments, criticisms to this long-delayed study of one of the most intriguing of bawdy songs in the English language, one that can be tracked back to the poet-playwright Ben Jonson's 1614 play, *The Humours of Bartholomew Fair*.

These worthies include Norm Cohen, Steve Gardham, Dick Greenhaus, Jonathan Lighter, Steve Roud, Abby Sale, Paul Stamler and Mike Williams, not to mention those acknowledged as my co-authors, Richard Reuss and John Patrick, who surely contributed the majority of the versions and variants assembled in the following pages.

Finally, let me also acknowledge the original theory proposed by a most difficult Gershon Legman — who took every opportunity to scorn my pioneering publication, *The Erotic Muse* — in his monumental two-volumes of annotations of the songs collected by Vance Randolph, published as *Roll Me in Your Arms* and *Blow the Candles Out*. It is Legman's theory that I have set out to prove. — Ed Cray

I. THE SONG

It is probably as well known as any bawdy rugby song — a redundancy, to be sure. Various verses circulate as widely known jokes. Its chorus has nothing to do with the verses; indeed, for the moment, the chorus remains something of a mystery as to its origins.

We're off to see the Wild West Show,
Elephants and the kangaroos,
Never mind the weather,
As long as we're together,
We're off to see the Wild West Show.

Then follows a farrago of verses, many of them scatological, involving ever more unusual animals, birds and people, each described in the commanding or wheedling tones of a carnival "barker."

Beyond those oddities, it is possibly the oldest extant bawdy song, descended in a convoluted fashion from Elizabethan playwright, Ben Jonson, and his still-mounted comedy, "The Humours of Bartholomew Fair."

As it meanders its way through the centuries, picking up bits of dross and floss here and there, adapting itself to the times and troubles, "The Wild West Show" borrows willy-nilly from popular song, from folk traditions, from jokelore, and thereby fashions a piece of enduring bawdry.

II. THE FAIR AND THE PLAY

First apprenticed as a brickwright, then later taking up arms as a stalwart soldier for the Crown and, later still, as a poet and playwright, Ben Jonson (1572–1637) presented in 1614 the third of his three most popular comedies: *Volpone*, *The Alchemist*, and *The Humours of Bartholomew Fair*. The last is a satire on a comparative handful of the many who attend the fair on August 24, that is, St. Bartholomew's Day, in the town of Smithfield, essentially a nest of slaughterhouses and execution grounds in a northwestern suburb, immediately outside the old walls of London. (The date of the fair was later shifted generally to September 5.)

Jonson was "a writer of overshadowed greatness," to quote Francis Teague's *The Curious History of Bartholomew Fair*.[4] A contemporary of Shakespeare, of Donne, Spenser and Sydney, later generations apparently determined Jonson never quite measured up to those men.

Still Jonson was an acute observer of his times. "In his comedy of Bartholomew Fair, he [Jonson] is in a dense center of London life," to quote yet another critic.[5]

> Bartholomew Fair is the climactic play of Ben Jonson's great comic period. Using the fair as a symbolic representation of religious, social, and political conflicts in Jacobean England, Jonson satirizes Puritans, fortune hunters, country bumpkins, and inept representatives of the justice system, along with sharpsters and con men who flock to the fair. This edition is the first to use the findings of feminist scholarship in examining the play's concern with forced marriage, pregnancy, sexual commerce, and widowhood.[6]

Henry Morley concluded, "Another very noticeable in this comedy is the very vivid of the characters through whom the satirist amuses himself with the follies of the Fair. They are many and various, yet every one of them is defined sharply, and they all go through a maze of misadventure without causing the least confusion to the witness of their huge bewilderment. In this respect, Bartholomew Fair is not excelled by any of Ben Jonson's works."[7]

Those at the fair in Jonson's play include, among many others, Littlewit, a proctor or student monitor; the Lady Littlewit, otherwise known as Win-the-fight; Littlewit's mother-in-law; her Puritan mentor/consort Zeal-of-the-Land Busy; as well as the wealthy Bartholomew Cokes, a noodle-head. All are a playwright's stereotypes.

> The characters themselves provide a kind of setting, for everyone in the first act wants something he does not have. John and Win Littlewit want to see John's puppet play and to escape Puritan restraints in having a good time; Dame Purecraft, Winwife and Grace all want to get married; Quarlous wants sport; Waspe wants to quarrel; Busy wants to eat and prophesy; and Dame Overdo simply wants to have a serene existence in which everyone agrees.[8]

"Humour," as Jonson defined it in his play *Everyman Out of His Humour*, was an attitude of personal independence, in a man not one to toady, a man unafraid, a man disdainful of self-serving gain; and a man ready to speak his mind whatever the consequences. The satire lies in the fact that none of the characters in the play possess those qualities.

As was the custom of his times, Jonson inserted a ballad in Act III for the ballad seller — ironically named Nightingale — entitled "A Caveat for Cutpurses." Though it would not survive in oral tradition, it remains the first song to be linked to the play, or incorporated into the play. That song begins:

My masters and friends, and good people, draw near,
And look to your purses, for that I do say;
And though little money in them you do bear,
It cost more to get, than to lose in a day,
You oft have been told,
Both the young and the old,
And bidden beware of the cut-purse so bold...[9]

Viewing the play in 1661, when *Bartholomew Fair* was revived, Samuel Pepys was decidedly ambivalent: "...to the Theater and there saw *Bartholomew faire*, the first time it was acted nowadays. It is [a] most admirable play and well-acted; but too much profane and abusive." Apparently Pepys was quite shocked by Jonson's assault on Puritanism.[10] He would later change his mind.

Sometime after 1661 and the Restoration, there was an apparent decline in the number of productions of *Bartholomew's Faire*. The Puritan "menace" was no more, the crown stood restored, and all was well with the English world. Nonetheless, broadsides delivered as "Bartholomew Fairings" waged political war across Puritan-Cavalier borders, this the dominant means of political posturing, even after the Restoration.[11]

In the first quarter of the 18th century, Jonson's play again found favor, though critics of the day deemed it of minor importance.[12] "Its eighteenth-century popularity was short-lived," Teague concluded.[13] For some 200 years, Teague estimated, the play lay forgotten. "*Bartholomew Fair*, in some ways the most characteristic of Jonson's plays, was simply the first to die."[14]

Not so the fair itself.

According to one student of London's amusements, the fair reached its zenith at the beginning of the 18th century. Extended to a two-week run, Bartholomew Fair morphed into a major presentation of theatrical entertainments. While the stage's celebrated actors had earlier disdained performing at the fair, eventually the lure of great receipts persuaded even those worthies to enjoy the fruits of a two-week run in a comedy especially written for presentation at the annual fair.[15]

By mid-century, the cry of the straight-laced was once more abroad in the land. The fair again was shortened once more to three days, ending any possibility of a financially successful theatrical run. Theatrical companies returned to their theatres.

In their place came touring "wilde beaste" shows, menageries of rare animals not often seen in captivity. As early as 1702, wrote William Boulton, "The good people of Smithfield were regaled with the sight of 'a tyger warranted to pluck the feathers from a fowl.'" Boulton continued, "A year or two later much excitement was occasioned by the appearance of a menagerie which, from a naive advertisement, we gather included such rarities as the 'Noble Cashaware brought from the Island of Java in the East Indies.... He eats iron, steel, and stones, and he hath two spears grows [sic] by his side." Later, Boulton notes, would come "two rattlesnakes, one of very large size, and rattles that you may hear him a quarter of a mile almost..." Then there was the "bovine curiosity or double cow... and a surprising young mermaid, taken on the shores of Aguapulca, that the generality of mankind believe there is no such thing." Sixpence admission would disabuse the skeptic of any doubt.[16]

Throughout the 18th century, the promoters' flights of fancy soared. There was "the eagle of the sun that takes the loftiest flight of any bird that flies," Boulton added, "the panther from Turkey on which there thousands of spots, and no two of a likeness; pelicans that suckle their young on their hearts' blood from Egypt; the noble vulture cock, having the finest tallons [sic] of any bird that seeks its prey..."[17]

"It was a happy state of society, we think, which could find continued amusement in such sights as these," Boulton continued. "But as the last [18th] century drew to its close, the naïveté of the audiences diminished, and dramatic effect apparently became necessary even in the menagerie."[18]

Through the 19th century the play gathered occasional performances, never quite forgotten despite its reputation as a sordid piece of work. Yet the play and the fair were not quite forgotten. William Wordsworth turned his attention to the fair itself, chronicling with tongue-in-cheek humor the wonders of the fair he recalled from an 1802 visit to the fair:

> All moveables of wonder, from all parts,
> Are here — Albinos, painted Indians, Dwarfs,
> The Horse of Knowledge, and the learned Pig,
> The Stone-eater, the man that swallows fire,
> Giants, Ventriloquists, the Invisible Girl,
> The Bust that speaks and moves its goggling eyes,
> The Wax-work, the Clock-work, all the marvelous craft
> Of modern Merlins, Wild Beasts, Puppet Shows,
> All out-o'-the-way, far-fetched, perverted things,
> All freaks of nature, all Promethean thoughts
> Of man, his dullness, madness and their feats,
> All jumbled up together, to compose
> A Parliament of Monsters.[19]

Well before the turn of the 19th century, the fair had become a magnet for thieves, cutpurses, whores, and any number of false coiners. It would finally be throttled by Victorians protesting its hedonistic proclivities in 1855. So ended a run of 720 years' duration. (There was no fair in the years of the Great Plague and Fire.)

III. LEGMAN'S THEORY

In 1964, Gershon Legman initially hypothesized that the clutch of songs describing "The Humours of Bartholomew Fair" was related to the much later bawdy song(s) known variously as "The Wild West Show" or sometimes "Larry, Turn the Crank."[20]

Four years later, in his "first series" of *Rationale of the Dirty Joke*, he repeated his theory.[21]

Despite a substantial and suggestive list of citations, in *Southern Folklore Quarterly* he seemingly backed off his theory, stating the cante-fable was "of Nineteenth Century origin."[22]

Then he once again reversed his field; in a letter to Richard Reuss, written on July 21, 1975, he reaffirmed that "The Hamburg Show," yet another variant of "The Wild West Show," was indeed related to "The Humours of Bartholomew Fair."

"Beyond 1840," Legman wrote, "I can only suggest the tradition (no texts) implied in Ben Jonson's play 'Bartholomew Fair' (c. 1610).... You will have observed that Ashton's and the 1840 text are called 'Humours of Bartelmy [St. Bartholomew's] Fair,' which gives a key to the milieu." (Legman's was a veiled suggestion that the lower classes had coopted the genre.)[23]

IV. THE CHAIN

This monograph is the first to take up Legman's conjectures. Moreover, given the all-embracing sweep of the Internet denied to that earlier generation, the task is made so much easier. Furthermore, Legman never considered the possibility of other influences on the cante-fable that was to become a 20th-century rugby song generally known as "The Wild West Show." There is much to be learned about the sweep and interaction of "folk" to "pop," or back again.

By 1799, no fewer than sixteen songs — and perhaps more yet to be discovered — were inspired by the fair. Back and forth, in a wicked war of wits, the songs centered on first the fair itself, then on the performers or acts, and finally on those who attended the fair.

In 1809, Charles Matthews refocused on the performers once more, but cast his song as a cante-fable, that is, a story that intermixed song with spoken dialogue. The Matthews text printed of that year is the first to introduce a "barker" or celebrant of the play.[24]

Bartholomew Fair

A popular Comic Ballad.
Sung by Mr. Matthews, with universal applause, at the Theatre Royal,
    Haymarket — Season 1809.

Come bustle, neighbour Prig,
Buckle on your Sunday wig;
In our Sunday clothes so gaily,
Let us strut up the Old Bailey.
Oh! the Devil take the rain;
Perhaps may never go again:
See the shows have begun, — O rare O!

Remember, Mr. Suip [sic, for Snip]
To take care of Mrs. Snip —
That's the little boy from Flanders,
And that there's Master Saunders!
Stand aside, and we'll have a stare O!
High down, O down, derry, derry, down,
O the humours of Bartlemy Fair O!

(Spoken) — Valk up, ladies and gentlemen — here's the vonderful birds and *beasteses* from Bengal in the *Vest* Indies. Here, Ma'am, only look at this beautiful *hanimal* — no two spots on his body alike — it's out of the power of any *limmer* to describe him — measures fifteen feet from the snout to the tail, and fifteen from the tail to the snout — grows an inch and a half every year, and never comes to his proper growth. — [sic] Turn him up there with a long pole.
High down, &c.

When the fair is at the full, in gallops a mad bull,
Puts the rabble to the rout, lets all the lions out;
Down falls Mrs. Snip, with a monkey on her hip —
We shall all be swallowed up, I declare O.
    Roaring boys — Gilded toys
    Lollipops — Shilling hops
    Tumble in — Just begin
    Cup and balls — Wooden walls
    Gin and bitters — Apple fritters
    Shins of beef — Stop thief!
    Lost shoes — Kangaroos
    O Polly — Where's Molly?
    Bow wow — What a row!
    High down, &c.

Now the beasts with hungry tooth, in anger 'tack the booth;
Away affrighted run birds and eagles of the sun,
Down tumbles trot-legg'd Rolla, who tips 'em the blue holla.[25]
Poor Cora's in the mud — O rare O.

(Spoken.) — Here, valk up ladies and gentlemen. — Here's the wonderful kangaroo from *Bottom-house* Bay. — Here's the vonderful large baboon, that danced a Paddy-dow, and play'd at leap-frog with the celebrated *Muster Barrington* [sic, for *Mister? Or Master?*] Here's the vonderful cow, that can't live on the land, and dies in the vater; the vonderful sun eagle, the hotter the sun the higher he flies. — Billy, run stuff a blanket in that hole, or the little boys vill peep for nothing. — Here! here! here! valk in! — suppose you think this man's alive, he's no more alive than you are. — Now's your time to see that vonderful vooden Roscius, Mr. Punch, for the small charge of one penny. — *(Mimicking Punch.)*

High down, O down, derry, derry, down,
What whirligigs of Bartlemy Fair O!

This is plainly satirical. Still there are a number of elements that suggest lines in the contemporary rugby song: "Devil take the rain" ("Never mind the weather"); tortured geography ("Bengal in the West Indies"); "no two spots on his belly alike" (the leopard); the bull (sometimes a monkey in later versions) that lets the lions out, scattering the crowd; the kangaroo from Bottom-house Bay (Botany Bay); the sun eagle (almost unchanged in current versions); the command to "stuff a blanket" lest "the boys peep for nothing."

Thirty years later, Mr. Matthews was still performing a greatly extended version of the "The Humours of Bartholomew Fair" adapted as "The Humours of a Country Fair."[26]

…Spoken.] Walk up, walk up, and see the wonderful Anarabaracabaradaliana, the great Physioner from Bengal in the *Vest Hingus*; he possesses the most unparalleled, inestimable, and never-to-be-matched medicines; and can cure anything incident to humanity from *a corn* up to *consumption!* we have a long list of cures performed by his grand eliptical, Asiatical, panticarical, nervius cordial, but will only read you three out of three-thousand, the whole of which it would be tedious to read to you — this is one: — "Sir, I was cut in half in a saw pit, cured with *one* bottle." — "Sir, I was jammed to death in a linseed oil mill, cured with *two* bottles." Now comes the most wonderful of all: — "Sir, venturing too near the powder mills at Faversham, I was, by a sudden explosion, blown into a million atoms; by this unpleasant I was rendered unfit for my business (a banker's clerk), but hearing of your grand eliptical, Asiatical, panticurical, nervius cordial, I was persuaded to make essay thereof, the first bottle united my strayed particles, the second animated my shattered frame, the third effected a radical cure, the fourth sent me home to Lombard-street, to count sovereigns, carry out bills of acceptance, and recount the wonderful effect of your grand eliptical, Asiatical, panticurical nervius cordial, that cures all diseases incident to humanity." — Twenty-four ballads for a *half*penny, four and twenty for a *harf*penny consisting of the following: "Within a Mile of Edinburgh;" "Drops of Brandy;" "Cast thine eyes, my love, around;" "The Old Commodore;" "*Gin* a body meet a body;" with "London now is out of town;" sung by me and my partner: Strike up Poll, and tip 'em the curl. *(Sings first verse of "London Now, &c.).*

Those in fairs who take delight,
In shows, and seeing every sight,
Dancing, singing and a fight,
    At a Country fair.
Boys by mamma's treacle fed,
With cakes and spicy gingerbread,
On every body's toes they tread,
    All at a Country fair.
Monkeys mounting camels' backs,
For prizes there men jump in sacks,
And others drinking quarts of max,
    And think that that's your sort.
Corks are drawing, glasses jingle,
Trumpets, drums together mingle,
Till your heads completely tingle,
    Which quite completes the sport.

Spoken:] Walk up, walk up, here is the Emperor of all the Conjurors, and Prince Regent of Houximepoksimehocopocococo, he shall take a red hot poker and thrust it into a barrel of gunpowder, and it will not go off; he will then load a blunderbuss with some of the *dentical* [sic] powder as would not explode, charged with twelve leaden bullets, which he will fire full in the face of any of the spectators, as pleases, without them being ever the worser, he will take the footman of any lady or gentleman and hang him up to the ceiling of the room, where he will let him hang, till he is requested by the company to let him down; he will borrow five or six shillings from any of the company, which he will never return to them, and all for his private use and emolument, without any other motive whatever. Now, my little dears, you have seen that, and the next *shall* be something else; now you have the representation of the taking of *Hallgiers*, by Lord Sir Issac Pelhoe, Esq., who was made Knight of Bath *and* Bristol for this very performance; look to the right, my little dears, and you'll see the treacherous Turks *a*loading of their guns and the poor Christian slaves asarving out the red hot balls with their naked hands; there you see the Turkey interpreter, Salami, entreating for to go below, to save his long beard, *which* he is afraid will be shot of [sic] by the cannon balls; look a little further and you will see a Mussellman blown up in the air into a million of anatomies; now, my little dears, look to the left and you'll see in the middle of the ocean, the mast of a three decker man of war, with three British seamen clinging to it, *for* to save their lives and to keep up the allegory of Britannia rules the waves. Ten a penny sausages, ten a penny sassages. Bless me, they smell very nice, and look very nice, don't they. Yes, I never eat any, but I should like [—] I am not hungry now — thought what you are made of, Mr. Doleful. I don't know, I have often meant to taste them myself, but never had the *risolution* to try one of 'em, there's a sort of prejudice, I've heard some people say, they're made of — but I never mention it unless I'm certain, though it's a curious coincidence, I lost my dog Pincher on this very spot last week. Ladies and gentlemen, walk up, and see the most surprise appearance in the whole fair, by the three brothers[,] Hali, Muley, and Hassan, from the Caribbee Islands, of which I am a native myself; Hali will take a lighted torch in his hand, and jump down the throat of his brother, Muley, who will in his turn jump down the throat of his brother Hassan, and though Hassan the elder, is encumbered with the weight of his two brothers Halu and Muley, he will take another torch, throw a flip flap and jump down his own throat, leaving the spectators completely in the dark.

Yes, I own 'tis my, &c.

Hali, Muley, and Hassan introduce at least one new feat that carries on to the present day: the snake and the ostrich, or the bird which flies in ever decreasing circles until it flies into his own anal orifice. Additionally, there is a suggestion of a peep or raree show in the last monologue.

But then, the path to "The Wild West Show" sharply detours.

Van Amburgh's Menagerie

For a short history of Issac Van Amburgh's career as an animal trainer, see the chronological entry (below) at 1839. Suffice here to say that Van Amburgh was so celebrated as an entertainer that a popular song, written by W.J. Wetmore, M.D., circulated both in sheet music and in multiple songsters. Its text runs:

Vanamburgh's [sic] Menagerie[27]

Old Vanamburgh [sic] is the man that runs all these [']ere shows,
He goes into the lion's den and shows you all he knows,
He sticks his head in the lion's mouth and holds it there a while,
Then he pulls it out again and turns around and smiles.

CHORUS:
The elephant now moves round, the music begins to play,
Them boys around the monkeys' cage had better keep away.

The first is the African polar bear, oft called the iceberg's daughter,
Has been known to eat six tons of ice and call for soger water.
He wades in the river up to his knees, not fearing any harm,
You may growl and snarl all you please, but he don't care a darn.

The hyena in the next cage, most wonderful to relate,
Got awful hungry the other night and ate up his female mate.
Don't go near his cage; he will hurt you little boys,
For when he's mad he wags his tail and makes an awful noise.

The next is the anaconda boa-constrictor, called the anasabrunity,
He can eat up a toad or an elephant and is noted for his great longility;
He can swallow his head, crawl through himself, come out with great facility,
And tie himself in a big bow-knot and wink with great agility.

The monkey in the next cage is cuffing his little brother,
He's not to blame for doing that, for he learned it of his mother.
The skin of his face is drawn so tight, and covered all over with marks,
That when he winks, he's sure to gape, and when he gapes, he winks.

The last is the eagle, awful bird from the highest mountain tops,
Has been known to eat up little birds and here his history stops;
The performance can't go on, there is too much noise and confusion,
If the ladies give them monkeys fruit, it will injure their constitution.

Most important, the Wetmore song establishes a sequence of animals in cages. That alone would be sufficient to set this song among "The Wild West" precursors. The lines about the tight skin may be the inspiration, or a sanitized rewrite of the commonly found verse that when the bird winks, it wanks, and when it wanks, it winks. Furthermore, the Wetmore version/rewrite carries a verse in which an animal swallows itself.

It does seem clear that the composer had heard or come across a printing of one or more of the extant "Humours" songs.

Similarly, the originally British popular song, "The Royal Wild Beast Show" — dated to 1870 — has contributed to the tangle of songs known as "The Wild West Show."

The Royal Wild Beast Show[28]

Come stand aside, good people all, and hear what I've to say,
But let the little dears come up, what's going for to pay.
At all the courts in Europe we are reckon'd quite the go,
Then pay your sixpences and see the Royal Wild Beast Show.

CHORUS:
The camomiles, the crocodiles, and all that you could wish;
The mice and rats, and tabby cats, and other kinds of fish;
A dozen sphinxes upside down, and standing in a row,
It's only sixpence each to see the Royal Wild Beast Show.

The first one is the kangaroo, you'll know him by his hump;
The next's the hippopotamus, you ought to see him jump.
The third's the alligator and he's such a one to crow,
He wakes us every morning in the Royal Wild Beast Show.

That pretty thing's the oozley bird, the other one's his aunt,
The third we call the pelican, the next the peli*cant;*
The other one's the solon [sic, for solan] goose — you musn't call out bo!
Or you will hurt his feelings in the Royal Wild Beast Show.

The donkey in the corner with the tiger on his arm,
Comes from *Ass*yria, where once his father kept a farm;
The billy goat that's dressed in pink and walking rather slow,
Is very *horn*imental in a Royal Wild Beast Show.

The tortoise, famous for his speed, unequal'd by a horse;
The parrot, too, who talks in *polly*-syllables, of course;
The raging elephants that roar when stormy winds do blow,
Are also represented in the Royal Wild Beast Show.

The next one is a mighty ape, indeed, I tell you true,
It's only natural he should "go walking in the Zoo;"
Our stock of monkeys, you'll observe, at present is but low —
They are so plentiful outside the Royal Wild Beast Show.

The last's the boa-constrictor, who eats all he finds about —
Why, who's been fool enough to let the nasty crittur [sic] out?
He's somewhere underneath the chairs, hi! mind your legs, hullo!
He's very quick in clearing out the Royal Wild Beast Show.

The "oozley bird" will turn up in at least one later version of "The Wild West Show" while a boa constrictor replaces a bull or monkey clearing out the crowds at the end of the song. At a guess, the Lee-Green team that wrote "The Royal Wild Beast Show" had heard or read an earlier text of "Bartholomew Fair."

Their song enjoyed multiple press runs in the years after 1870, with or without credit to either Messers Green or Lee.

Meanwhile, Dr. Wetmore's "Van Amburgh" text apparently dropped from copyright status into the turbulence of folk tradition. As "The Menagerie," the Boston publishing house of Oliver Ditson in 1876 credited a rewrite to one C.T. Miller, of Providence, Rhode Island.[29]

Come all and listen to me, and as you stand around,
I will show you the greatest menagerie that ever was in town.
We are here in a great cloth tent with cages round the sides.
There is the elephant Emeline over there that everybody rides.

Von Humbug is the man that owns all these 'ere shows.
He'll get into the lion's den ami [sic, for and] show you all he knows.
He'll put his head in the lion's mouth, and hold it there a while.
He'll take it out again pretty soon, and then look around and smile.

That leopards never change their spots he'll prove to be a blunder.
He'll make them lay in this 'ere spot, then change to that spot yonder.
He moves among the savage brutes, not fearing any harm.
They may growl and snarl all they please but he don't care a cent [*sic, for* show alarm? Give a darn?]

With the wonderful Rhino-noceros [sic], the program does begin.
He wades in water up to his knees and then wades out again.
That horn on top of his nose is a toothpick he cannot use
Except to pick up human beings and shake 'em right out of their shoes.

Here's the giraffe-camel-leopard with a great long spotted throat,
His head's so high and out of town, that he ain't allowed to vote.
With forelegs long and hind legs short, he scampers o'er the plain.
And his long legs often rest themselves till the short catch up again.

Here's the wonderful Dromedary, double-breasted in the back,
You see his toes are cracked in two so he always toes the crack.
When in Noah's ark, they got him mad, and drove him round and round,
And Drommy got his back up, and never got it down.

And here's the golden eagle, America's proud bird.
They say he "shouts for liberty," but he never says a word.
He puts his head beneath his wing, makes seventy-six gyrations.
Then whistles "Yankee Doodle' and shrieks the variations.

That zebra standing in the next cage there, too sleepy to kick or bite,
Has a thousand marks across his back and Harry [sic, for nary] one alike.
The skin on his face is drawn so tight, and covered up with marks,
That when he gapes, he's sure to wink, and when he winks he gapes.

The next, the African polar bear, often called the iceberg's daughter,
Has been known to eat ten tons of ice, then call for soda water.
The performance can't go on, there's too much noise and confusion.
Ladies, don't give those monkeys fruit; it will injure their constitution.

That speckled snake in the blanket there, noted for great longevity,
Is Anna Maria Condor Boa Constrictor snake, called Anaconda for brevity.
She will tie herself in thirteen knots, and eat with great voracity,
Swallow her head, turn inside out, and go backwards with great alacrity.

That kangaroo that is hopping about, and cuffing his little brother,
Is not to blame for doing so, for he learned it of his mother.
He measures eighteen feet you see, I measure with this cane.
He's nine feet long from head to tail, and nine feet back again.

Now, John, stir up those monkeys, and, Jimmie, feed the bear,
Make Christopher Columbus and Washington fight, and pull one another's hair.
Here is the monkey[,] "Drooping Lily," of all her friends bereft,
The ourang outang is looking love at her, with his right hand "over the left."[30]

Here is the Crying Hyena, of the insect tribe, most wonderful of all,
He makes night hideous and daylight too by his everlasting squall.
With tearful eyes he roams about, and snaps at all the boys,
And once in fifteen minutes makes this remarkable noise. (Yell)

The last is the vulture — awful bird — from the highest mountain tops,
He stuffs himself with little birds, and here his history stops.
The audience will please retire. The hyena is getting mad.
The boys have got the monkeys cross, and Emeline is feeling bad.

Thus, "The Van Amburg Show" and its derivative "Menagerie" are entangled within "The Wild West Show."

The Raree-Show Thread

Enter yet another contributor to "The Wild West Show," this is from *A Collection of Humorous, Dramatic and Dialect Selections* published in 1878. These are generally grouped as "Raree-Shows," that is, "rarity shows," and defined by some variant of the command "Larry [or Boy], turn the crank!" Compiler James Burdette is credited for this parlor-presentable "The Irishman's Panorama" that contains the command: "James, move the crank! Larry, music on the bagpipes!"[31] Four more times, the narrator commands: "Move the crank," a command will most often appear as "Larry, turn the crank!"

William C. Smith offers the first suggestion that a bawdy song was evolving in his boyhood recollections as printed in *Queen City Yesterdays: Sketches of Cincinnati in the Eighties*: The barker "…would call out, 'Larry, turn the crank,' when his assistant would run in another slide. His spiel was often parodied by the more sophisticated of that generation and such parodies in time trickled down to the lower age levels and provided amusement for youths of the mature age of thirteen. It is regrettable that such parodies cannot be reprinted…"[32]

About the same time, surreptitiously, there appeared "The Stag Party," an unpaginated, though typeset, anonymous publication, sometimes attributed to journalist-poet Eugene Field. Legman has dated it to 1888 because of a reference to the presidential campaign of that year.[33]

Three copies are known to exist, according to Legman; the copy below will be found is from the library of the Kinsey Institute at Indiana University, for which Legman was a paid "smut hunter." In this typescript copy, a Yankee sells to an Irish Californian a "peep show." For a week, the Yankee travels with the show, delivering the patter, until the Irishman says he has learned the spiel. He then hires a lad to travel with him, instructing the boy that his cue is, "Boy, turn the crank."

The first panel of the show depicts Adam and Eve in the Garden of Eden, followed successively by Daniel in the lion's den, Noah's ark, then the angel warning Balaam not to curse the Israelites. That then is followed by Lot incestuously enjoying intercourse with one of his two daughters, and the show concluding, finally, with Joseph and Potiphar's wife. The five-minute narrative ends with the customer and the Irishman fighting. (A copy of the full text will be found below under the rubric 1888.)

Loosely dated to the 1890's, a recorded text by Willy Smith — recording under the pseudonym of James White — was retrieved on the compact disc "Actionable Offenses: Indecent Phonograph Recordings from the 1890S" [sic] with accompanying liner notes by Eric Nuzum, and additional contributions by Meagan Hennessey and Richard Martin.[34] The recorded text runs with the liner notes' advice that "nineteenth-century audiences would have understood that Casey is exhibiting a 'moving panorama' a series of artworks on a long canvas mounted on two spools."

Now Add a Chorus and a Criticism

The year 1908 furnishes the first report of what has become the now virtually inevitable chorus of "The Wild West Show." It is attached to a cheer for athletes at a normal school in Michigan:

"Where are we going?[35]
Oh, we're going to the Hamburg Show,
To see the elephant and the kangaroo,
And we'll all stick together through rain and stormy weather,
For we're going to see the whole show through."

With that, later versions of "The Van Amburg Show" and its derivative "Menagerie" are bound to the later "The Wild West Show."

In the June, 1925, issue of *The American Mercury*, gadfly critic H.L. Mencken scored "folk-lorists" as "schoolmarms, male or female, and their interest is concentrated on more seemly heroes and more gentle legends…. [T]hey have given little attention to the geste of Bunyan and none at all to such noble American sagas as that of Larry and the panorama. Who, having heard any part of the latter, will ever forget it? 'This strange beast, ladies and gentlemen, is the laughing hyeneus…. What's he got to laugh about, I'll be damned if I know!' And the ibex, pursuing the female of the species through the primeval forest! And the cassowary! And the astounding bird that laid the bricks for Cheops' pyramid! The epic of Larry has been reduced to paper by more than one exhilarated scribe, but I don't believe that it has ever been printed, even privately." [36]

This monograph addresses Mencken's gripe.

V. THE CHRONOLOGY

1614

In this year, as Claude Simpson notes in his *The British Broadside Ballad and Its Music*, the Stationers Corporation licensed "Roome for Companie, here comes Good Fellowes. To a pleasant new tune."[37]

Basing his opinion on a seventeenth century lute tablature at Trinity College, Cambridge, Simpson found the melody under the title "Roome for Cuckolds." He theorized that this might have been the original title, a title later denatured as "Company." This version of that song shifts the focus from Jonson's comparative handful of those attending the fair to the masses which thronged to the fair grounds. The text of "Roome for Companie" runs:

CHORUS:
Room for company, here comes good fellows,[38]
Room for company in Bartholomew Fair.

Cobblers and broom-men, jailers and loom-men,
Botchers and tailors, shipwrights and sailors,
Paviers, bricklayers, potters and brickmakers,
Pinners and pewterers, plummers and fruiterers
Room for company, well may they fare.

Pointers and hosiers, sailmen and clothiers,
Horse-coursers, carriers, barbers and weavers,
Colliers and carvers, barbers and weavers,
Sergeants and yeomen, farmers and ploughmen,
Room for company, well may they fare.

Bellfounders, fellmongers, pumpmakers,
Glassmakers, chamberlains and matmakers,
Collarmakers, needlemakers, buttonmakers, fiddlemakers,
Fletchers and bowyers, drawers and sawyers,
Room for company, well may they fare.

Cutpurses and cheaters, and bawdy-house keepers,
Punks, aye, and panders, and cashier'd commanders,
Room for company, ill may they fare,
Room for company, here comes good fellows
Room for company, well may they fare.

1638

Hyder E. Rollins cites "Bartholomew Fare' as licensed for publication on August 21, 1638. Rollins is uncertain of the actual content, but hypothesizes it may be "A Description of Bartholomew Fair" beginning: "You Bartholomew Tapsters I first do advise."[39]

1639

Rollins (see entry for 1638) cites the licensing of "A Bartholomew Fairing" granted to one Richard Harper on September 23, 1639.

1661

Morley's *Memoirs of Bartholomew Fair* laments "the license fashionable in the days of Charles the Second." He mentions a tract "of six pages of filth 'by Peter Aretine,' [properly Aretino] printed for 'Theodofus Microcosmus,' a sequel to five pamphlets of which the contents are inexpressibly disgusting. The title of this pamphlet begins by promising 'Strange news from Bartholomew Fair;' the rest of it I do not care to quote. All to be learnt from it is, that in Duck Lane and Pye Corner were many dens of wickedness, that bawds were also thieves, that they were punished by whipping, and that there were still [Puritan] Zealots who came into the Fair."

Morley continues, noting that during the Restoration, the fair of three days' duration was extended to a fortnight, then again for six weeks' "riot of amusement."[40]

1665-66

The year of the Great Plague "was no year for Bartholomew Fair."[41] Nor was the next, marked instead by caution lest the plague return. That year too the Great Fire of London broke out on September 2, flames racing along a two-mile front, smoke casting a pall over a fifty-mile area. Had the fair been running, the temporary booths of the fairgrounds would have been destroyed.

1667

The fair resumes, this year featuring a "Wonder of Nature," a 16-year-old girl, her body misshapen, just 18 inches in height, who could read, discourse, whistle and sing. Pepys attends the fair with his wife, "and there did see a ridiculous obscene little stageplay, called 'Marry Audrey,' a foolish thing, but seen by everybody…" From there the party moved on to applaud the rope-dancer, Jacob Hall, who was whispered to share the favors of the King's mistress, Lady Castlemaine.[42] Subsequently, Jacob Hall returned to Bartholomew Fair in 1679 with his company of slack rope dancers, now including "a Dutch dancer who did wonderful feats," according to one person who saw the performances. This is the first mention of Dutch dancers, who for another 175 years would perform at Bartholomew Fair.

ca. 1680

"Enough has been read of the story of the Fair to show that it was as truly as the House of Commons, part of the Representation of the English people; not, indeed, its Lower, but its Lowest House."[43]

1682

Morley's *Memoirs of Bartholomew Fair* quotes from "Wit and Drollery: Jovial Poems," published in 1682, the following:

Here's that will challenge all the Fair[44]
Come buy my nuts and damsons and Burgamy pears!
Here's the woman of Babylon, the Devil and the Pope,
Here's the little girl just going on the rope!
Here's *Dives and Lazarus* and the *World's Creation,*
Here's the *Tall Dutch Woman,* the like's not in the Nation.
Here's the Booths where the High Dutch Maid is,
Here are the bears that dance like any ladies;
Tat, tat, tat, tat, says little penny Trumpet;
Here's Jacob Hall, that does so jump it, jump it;
Sound Trumpet, sound, for silver Spoon and Fork,
Come, here's your dainty Pig and Pork.

1682

In his *A Little Book of Songs and Ballads*, Edward F. Rimbault reprints four songs that deal with Bartholomew Fair. He culled these from a manuscript volume of "old Songs" dated on the flyleaf 1682. The songs include:

A Song on Bartholomew Fair[45]

Bonny lads and damsels,
Your [sic] welcome to our booth;
We're now come here on purpose
Your fancies for to sooth [sic]:
No heavy Dutch performers,
Amongst us you shall find;
We'll make your lads good humour'd,
And lasses very kind:
Your dansens and filberds,
You're welcome here to crack;
But a glass of merry sack[,] boys,
Is a cordial for the back.

You may range about the fair,
New tricks and sights to see;
And when your legs are weary,
Pray come again to me:
There's thread-bare *Holofernes*,
Whom *Judith* long hath slain;[46]
With *Guy of Warwick, St. George*,
And *Rosamond's* fair dame:
You'll find some pretty puppets too,
With many a nickey-nack;
But a glass of jolly sack, boys,
Is a cordial for the back.

The houses being low too,
Some players hither come;
But if my stars deceive men [sic, for me?] not,
They soon will know their doom;
There's other pretty strollers,
That crowd upon us here,

That may have booths to let too,
Before their time I fear:
All these may prate and talk much,
Show tricks and bounce and crack;
But here's a glass of sack, boys,
That's a cordial for the back.

Come sit down then, brisk lads all,
A bumper to the king;
Old England let's remember,
May peace and plenty spring:
Let war no more perplex you,
Your taxes soon will end;
The soldiers all disbanded,
And each man love his friend:
Be merry then, carouse[, sic] boys,
See drawer what is't they lack;
And fetch a bottle neat boy,
That's a cordial for the back.

Rimbault notes in a footnote that in 1702 it was reported that those who attended the fair would see "the famous Dutch woman's side-capers, upright-capers, cross-capers, and back-capers on the tight rope. She walks too on the slack rope, which no woman but herself can do."[47]

1685

In this year Sir Robert Southwell wrote to his son some observations about Bartholomew Fair:

The main importance of this fair is not so much for merchandize, and the supplying what people really want; but as a sort of Bacchanalia, to gratifie the multitude in their wandring [sic] and irregular thoughts.... Here you see rope dancers get their living merely by hazarding their lives, and why men will pay money and take pleasure to see such dangers, is of separate and philosophical consideration.... Others, if born in any monstrous shape, or have children that are such, here they celebrate their misery, and by getting of money forget how odious they are made....

There are various corners of lewdness and impurity… And how many robberies are beforehand committed on houses and high-ways to raise a stock against this licentious occasion! Here it commonly ends in quarrels and bloodshed, so that either chirurgeon is sent for to plaster up the wounds, or the constable to heal the peace, and truth breaking out among malefactors, Mr. Justice has sufficient grounds for his mittimus, and Captain Richardson [Keeper of the Old Bailey] favours them with house-room, and Mr. John Ketch [the hangman] conveys them at length to their long and deserved home.[48]

1687

Rimbault plucked this commentary regarding the cacophony of the fair "from a rare musical volume, entitled *The Second Part of the Pleasant Musical Companion*," published in 1687.

The Humours of Bartholomew Fair[49]

Here's that will challenge all the Fair:
Come buy my nuts and damsons, my Burgamy pear.
Here's the *Whore of Babylon*, the *Devil and the Pope:*
The girl is just going on the rope.
Here's *Dives and Lazarus,* and the *World's Creation:*
Here's the *Dutch Woman*, the like's not in the nation.
Here is the booth where the tall *Dutch Maid* is,
Here are the *bears* that dance like any ladies.
Tota, tota, tot, goes the little *penny trumpet,*
Here's your *Jacob Hall*, that can jump it, jump it.
Sound trumpet: a silver spoon and fork;
Come here's your dainty *Pig and Pork.*

From the same *Second Part of the Pleasant Musical Companion* (1687), Rimbault reprinted "The New Humours of Bartholomew Fair."[50]

Here are the rarities of the whole Fair,
Pimper-le-Pimp, and the wise Dancing Mare;
Here's valiant *St. George and the dragon,* a farce,
A girl of fifteen with strange moles on her a[rse]:
Here's Vienna beseig'd, a rare thing,
And here's *Punchinello* shown thrice to the king.

Ladies mask'd to the cloisters repair,
But there will be no raffling, a pise [piss?] on the Fair.[51]

1691

"An Auction of Whores, or The Bawds [sic] Bill of Sale, for Bartholomew Fair, Held in the Cloysters, near Smithfield." This song, credited to Michael Altham, was printed in London for N.H., who is not otherwise identified. Apparently at some countryside fairs, there was a practice of wife-selling, with accompanying ballads celebrating the sale.[52]

1700

Certainly, by 1700, Bartholomew Fair's cast of characters had firmed: acrobats of all types and feats, anatomical curiosities, and menageries, great and small. Add in panoramas, puppet shows retelling "The Creation of the World" or ever more elaborate stage plays, and the whole filled with teeming hordes of Londoners.

An Ancient Song of Bartholomew Fair[53]

In Fifty-five, may I never thrive if I tell you any more than is true,
To London she came, hearing of the fame of a Fair they call *Bartholomew*.

In Houses of Boards,[54] men walk upon cords, as easy as Squirrels crack filberds;
But the cut-purses they do bite and run away, but those I suppose are Ill-birds.

For a Penny you may zee [sic] a fine Puppet-play, and for two-pence a rare work of Art;
And a penny a cann [sic]; I swear a man may put six of them into a Quart.[55]

Their zights are so rich, is able to bewitch the heart of a very fine man-a;
Here's *Patient Grisel* here, and *Fair Rosamund* there, and the History of Susanna.

At *Pye-corner* end, mark well my good Friend, 'tis a very fine dirty place,
Where there's more Arrows and Bows, the Lord above knows, than was handled at *Chevy-Chase*.

At every door [waits] a Hag or a [sc]ore, and in *Hosier-lane*, if I ain't mistaken.
Such plenty there are, of w—es [whores], you'll have a pair, to a single Gammon of Bacon.

Then at *Smithfield-Bars*, 'twixt the ground and the stars, there's a place they call S*hoemaker's-Row,*
Where you may buy Shoes every day, or go bare-foot all the year I trow.

1701

A four-page chapbook printed for R. Hine entitled "A Walk to Smith-field: or a True Description of the Humours of *Bartholomew Fair,* with the many comical Intrigues and Frolicks that are acted in every *Booth* in the Fair, by Persons of All Ages and Sexes, from the Court Gallant to the Country Clown."[56]

The narrative contains such lines as "…I had an itching Fancy to see the Asses of both Sexes within the Wooden Tents of Iniquity, the whole Fair resembling nothing more than a fix't Camp… in so much that I found it difficult to stear my Course above three Yards in half an Hour's time, but having gain'd some Experience by my long continuance in the Crowd; I squeezed and drew in my Paunch between the fatt-bellied Females, just like a fatt Man thro a narrow Stile, so that with artificial Hipp work and Thigh work, I labour'd as hard as ever any furious Lover did to riggle [sic] himself between the Knees of a coy Mistries [sic, for Mistress]."

1705

"Roger in Amaze: or the country-mans [sic] ramble through Bartholomew-fair To the tune of The Dutch Woman's Jigg." Printed by and for A.M. and sold by J. Walter, at the hand and pen [sic] in High Holburn, London.[57]

1707

"The Cloyster in Bartholomew Fair or, the town mistress disguis'd. A poem." Printed for A. Banks, near Fleetstreet, London. An unseen copy is in the Swem Library, William and Mary College. Others are in Harvard Library, and the Newberry in Chicago.

1717

"Bartholomew Fair: an heroic-comical poem" is printed and sold in London by S. Baker, at the Black Boy and Anchor, in Pater-Noster Row. An unseen copy is in the Swem Library, William and Mary College.

1727

A new entertainment, the Ups-and-Downs — later to be known as a Ferris Wheel — was a feature of the fair that year. Just how it was powered a crude print reproduced in Morley does not make clear.[58]

1728

The year marked the first performances at the fair of John Gay's *The Beggar's Opera*. Plays were performed six times daily, which in itself would put a strain on singer and musician alike.[59]

1735

London's Court of Aldermen finally resolved that Bartholomew Fair "shall not exceed Bartholomew's Eve, Bartholomew's Day, and the Day after; and that during that time nothing but stalls and booths shall be erected for the sale of goods, wares, and merchandise, and no acting be permitted."[60]

1750

Plays creep back in, only to be banned again in 1750, then restored anew. Circa 1750–54, Morley notes "a famous Italian female Samson" is a major attraction. About the same time, he writes, appeared "the wonderful and astonishing Arabian Poney [sic] who could count the spots on cards and then tap them out with his hoof." Similarly, the animal could tap out the time on any gentleman's watch.[61]

1753

The fair is moved to begin on September 3, and to run for 11 days.

1760

Smithfield, previously outside the city walls, is swallowed by a growing London.

1762

The tumult of the fair is described in a six-stanza poem by George Alexander Stevens, published in this year as "A Description of Bartholomew Fair in London." Clearly, the fair had fallen on grievous times.

> …The taphouse roaring, and the mouthpieces bawling,
> Pimps, pawnbrokers, strollers, fat landladies, sailors,
> Bawds, bailiffs, jilts, jockies, [sic], thieves, tumblers, taylors [sic].[62]

1769

Both theatrical performances and Punch and Judy shows once again are banned. Seventy-two officers are appointed to make certain there was no gambling at the fair and places of refreshment are closed at eleven o'clock.[63]

ca 1770

Pidcock's Wild Beast Show succeeded Polito, followed by one Miles, all three "menageries" of rarely exhibited animals. Other curiosities in this decade included a giant hog, almost fourteen feet long; a six-legged ram; and a unicorn ram.[64]

1790

"A descriptive Poem, of Bartholomew-Fair, for the instruction and amusement of youth of both sexes… Written by Ben. Johnson, the younger." (London: Printed for H. Turpin, No. 104, St. John's Street, West Smithfield, 1790). Not seen.[65]

1793?

"The New Humours of Bartholomew Fair," originally a song, but without music and thereby reduced to a simple poem, makes mention of the taking of Valenciennes by the Duke of York in 1793.[66]

> Come lads and come lasses, now trip it away,
> To Bartholomew Fair, where there's sights fine and gay,
> There's Flockton and Jonas are shewing away.
>
> CHORUS:
> With their round abouts, kick up routs,
> Porcupine, gul'otine, shows so fine,

Sing derry, derry, derry, up and down.
Let's to Smithfield repair.

Flockton was a puppet-master, "one of the great showmen of Bartholomew Fair," according to Morley, who retired "with a small fortune" of 5000 pounds. Apparently Jonas, otherwise lost to history, was similarly employed.[66]

1798

A "newspaper wit" (to borrow Morley's term) wrote that the fair in this year boasted "some of the first actors, the first singers, the first dancers, the first horsemen in the whole world; ghosts, spectres, bluebeards, and bleeding nuns, descending amid flashes of rosin and ascending amid clouds of tobacco."[67]

1799

"Bartholomew Fair" or "The Humours of Smithfield"[68]
Sung by Mr. Johannot. Tune: The Pyeman [sic]

O Bartlemy, Bartlemy Fair;
That scene of confusion and frolic,
Such wonderful doings are there,
'Twould cure an old maiden of the cholic:
There's sausages frying in grease,
No one can dislike but a snarler,
Black puddings a penny a piece,
'Walk in and sit down in my parlour.'
   Ri um ti idity um, &c.

There's round-abouts, wild beasts, and monkies [sic],
And also the wonderful pig!
There's gentlemen riding on donkies [sic],
And gin for the ladies to swig:
There's conjurors, giants, and witches,
With — show 'em up, show 'em up there,
 There's gingerbread cocks, sir, and breeches,
And buttons a farthing a pair.
   Ri um ti idity um, &c.

O then if you walk but about,
There's "here is your nuts, up and win 'em,"
There's fighting both indoor and out,
And pockets with nothing within 'em;
There's fairings of every kind,
There's waggons, [sic] with coaches and six,
Aye, and what I wou'd have you to mind —
A great many *flight of hand tricks*.
   Ri um ti idity um, &c.

There's "Who's for a ride round the fair
Step into my coach, miss, and rest?"
"O no, sir, (says she), I declare,
I love a sweet up and down best."
There's fortunes told here in a trice,
For husbands for those that have tarried,
There's 'O then, I'm sure that is nice,
Dear me, how I long to be *married*.'
   Ri um ti idity um, &c.

1809

This is the *unprinted*, pivotal song/text, from which are descended contemporary versions of the commonly noted rugby song "The Wild West Show." Titled "Bartholomew Fair," it was performed by Charles Matthews in the play *Killing No Murder* by Edward Hook at the Little Theatre in the Haymarket. In the printed version text of the play, this was followed by the line: "Song/This song is private property, and cannot be published."[69]

The play was to debut on June 20, 1809, but was denied a license for performance before the premier because, as Hook wrote later, he intended to attack Methodist preachers "so that the lash of ridicule might well be applied to their backs."[70] Hook, who seemingly stood as a defender of the established Episcopal hierarchy, was a young, but sly and pugnacious, beginning playwright. He revised his play to remove the offending speeches, but replaced them with such lines as scored the censor himself or noted "what I must not mention."[71]

Since the revisions "touched neither on politics nor religion, the Examiner was unable to expunge them." The play debuted on August 29, 1809. Mr. Matthews played the lead of Buskin, as a trickster, a scamp, a scapegrace, scofflaw and deadbeat. It was a perfect part for an actor earning a reputation as a humorist. It was he who introduced the closing act of the play with the segueway lines that concern us here:

"[F]aith they have stopped — never mind. It will give me time to compose my spirits — for I have to go through to night [sic], as the showman at Bartelmy fair, damme, the very recollection of that scene of festivity gives me new life — 'tis the epitome of the world."[72]

1817

This is the first printing recovered of Mr. Matthews' "Bartholomew Fair." Significantly, it took eight years to find its way into print — as the broadside made clear. (Roud has numbered it in his index of broadsides as B41435.)

The Matthews cante-fable, and it is that for the first time, contains a handful of elements that make their initial appearance: "Devil take the rain," the misplacement of geographical locations, the clearing of the audience; the sun eagle; and stuffing a blanket in a hole so the boys won't see a show without paying.

1824

The British Minstrel and National Melodist: A Collection of the Most Esteemed and Popular English, Scottish and Irish Songs, etc. (London: Sherwood, Gilbert and Pipe, 1827), pp. 279–84, reprints "Humours of Bartholomew Fair," but without credit to Mr. Matthews. (This is still Roud ID number B41435 though greatly expanded.)

> Come bustle neighbour Prig
> Buckle on your flaxen wig;
> In our Sunday clothes so gaily,
> We'll strut up the Old Bailey;
> O the devil take the rain,
> We may never go again,
> See the shows have begun, oh rare oh!
>   Springing rattle,
>   Horned cattle,
>   Hot spice,
>   All so nice,

Fat ox,
Pit and box,
Eating fire,
Slack wire,
Tumble in,
Just begin, [sic]

Spoken.] — 'Valk up, valk up, ladies and *gemmen*, here's the most wonderful birds, wild *beastes and beastesses*, there ever was seen in the vorld, or any where else alive; and just arrived from *Benegal*, in the *Vest Indies*. Here is the wonderful sea cow that can't live in the water, and dies on the land, *to be seen alive*. Only look, marm, at this *ere butiful* hanimal, no less than two hundred spots on his body, no two alike, and *every von different*; it's out of the power of any *limmer* to describe him.' — 'Vell! positively, I never *saw'd* such a *bootiful* creatur [sic] in all my born days, positively, did you, sir?' — 'A d—d fine looking animal, 'pon my word, mem.' — 'I say, Master Showman, how long do you suppose this *ere* creature is?' — 'How long! Measures fifteen feet from the tail to the snout, and twelve feet from the snout to the tail; lives! oh dam'me, lives to the *hadvanced* age of *vone hundred ears* [sic]; grows an inch and a half every *hannual year*, and never comes up to his proper growth.' — 'Stir him up, stir him up, there, keeper, with a long pole.' — 'Oh law! pa, I is so very frightened; only hear how the *vild beastesses* roars; Oh, pray do take me out, daddy, or I shall be sick. Oh la! I thinks I feels one of the tame leopards *nawing* [sic] my shoulder and shin bones.' — 'Well, you shouldn't ha'e come.' — 'Oh! then let me get under the tail of your coat.' — 'There's the wonderful and surprising sun eagle, ladies and *gemmen*; the *hotterer* the sun is, the higher he flies; and *vone* day, the sun being *hotterer* than common, he *flied higherer* than usual, and burnt one of his left wings; and though it has never burnt before[,] it has always been burnt since.

Hey down, ho down, derry derry down,
What wonders at Bartlemy Fair, O!
Come, bustle Mister Dip
Take care of Mister Snip;
Aye[,] neighbours never fear,
Come along my pretty dear;
That there's Master Saunders,

That's the little Dwarf from Flanders,
Stand aside and let's have a stare O.
    Fine toys,
    Roaring boys,
    Learned pig,
    Where's my wig?
    All hit,
    Higher trot,
    Cups and balls,
    Wooden walls,
    Lollipops,
    Shilling drops.

Spoken.] — 'Oh, law! oh, law! I never was in such a *scroudge* in all my life. Bless me! bless me! how the folks do *squeedge*, to be sure; — I say, you sir, do you see what you're about?' — 'No, I don't, marm.' — 'Why, you're *pushing* the funny-bone in my *helbow* right through that *ere gemman's* back.' — 'Oh, I beg your pardon marm.' — 'Ah! you nasty, dirty, great, [sic] big, ugly, monstrous man, You've trod on my corn, you have' — 'How the devil was I to know you had corns in your shoes, and be d—'d to you; the next time you come to the fair, you'd better leave your corns at home.' — 'Well! Positively, Betty, since I was born.' — 'Valk in, valk in, ladies and gemmen, here's the vonderful learned dog, the most *bootifulest, littlest* hanimal that *never* was seen.; he possesses more *knowledge* than *Shakspur* [sic] or *Wirgil*, this is the last time, ladies and *gem'men* [sic], you may ever have an opportunity of seeing this surprising creature, and the charge is only a penny; if there's any more, let 'em walk up, we're just now going to begin.' *(another voice)* — 'Now's your time, now's your time; here's the *vonderful* nab that lives upon fire, and is always as cool as a *cowcumber*, he keeps a *veeving* manufactory in his mouth, sufficient to supply all the girls in the fair with ribbons: he is, ladies and *gemmen*, one of the *wonderfullest* men that ever you clapped your eyes upon; and if you are not satisfied after seeing him, your money shall be returned when you come out.' — 'Make *vay*, there, for that *ere* young lady with the *hour-glass waist* and *pigeon breast* to step up; this *vay*, marm, just going to begin.' —'Now, ladies and gentlemen, allow me to recommend you a *good article*, here's some of the finest *sassenges* that ever was seen; only valk-into [sic] my back parlour, marm, there's some of the genteelest company in this ere fair, I can assure you.[sic] (Holloa, there, Bill, drive the pigs out of the parlour, will you, and lay the cloth.) — Take a seat in the corner by that *ere sweep*, marm, I'll soon bring you the *sassengers.*' — 'I say, you sir, here's no more *musted* in this *ere* box.' — 'No' nor I beant gotten any pepper in this *ere*. [sic] 'Coming directly, *gemmen*, I'll shave you while the water boils.' — 'O! dear.' — 'What, my dear Mrs. Lincolnpooper, what the devil's the matter.' — 'Oh dear! Mr. Mashmeat, I feels some how [sic] all over uncommonly queer.' — 'Pon my word, marm, you look exceedingly pale in the face.' — ' I say, your *sassengers* is remarkably rich.' — 'Yes, they're always reckon'd very *flavorish*; but, my dear ma'am, I am sadly afraid you don't know what's in 'em and liave [sic, for have] *eated* too many.' — 'No, no, no, I haven't; I'm very much subject to bilious attacks, I've only *eat eleven and three quarters.*' — 'The devil! eleven and three-quarters, did you say? Oh, well, well, what a *gluttoness gut,* I think you needn't grumble, you've had your three *haporth.*' — 'Oh, oh, oh, I shall go into a fit, I shall be very sick, I shall faint, faint, faint, and go into *stirrics.*' — 'Now, my good lady, do come out; consider you're in the supper room.' — 'What the devil shall I do with this d—'d woman; she'll turn all the men's *stomaks.*' — (lady retches.) — 'Holloa, holloa, Jack! Jack, bring a mop and bason [sic], here's a lady rather —

Hey down, &c.
And when the fair is at the full
In gallops a mad bull,
Puts the rabble to the rout,
And lets the lions out;
Down tumbles Mrs. Snip,
With a monkey on her hip;
We shall all be swallow'd up, I declare, O!
    Murder, help!
    Leopards whelp,
    Lost shoes,
    Rainy weather,
    Jammed together,
    Stop thief,
    Yeo, ho,
    Here we go.

Spoken.] — 'This vay, [sic] this vay, for the players, the players; remember, ladies and *gemmen*, this is none of your paltry *conjuration*, for without *exaggeration* they're all *botheration*, and you can't gain from them the least *information* or *edification*. The title of our piece, ladies and gemmen, [sic] is "The Fall of the Usurper." It is the true *representation* of the events of a *nation*, which long has been held in high *estimation*, who sent a *deputation* to the head of the *nation*, but his power, you must know, was through *usurpation*. When he saw the *deputation* he was in great *consternation*, much *agitation*, and vast *tribulation*, and his eye balls swelled with high *indignation;* so without *procrastination*, or cool *deliberation*, he ordered the *deputation* to die by *starvation;* but, a bold *determination* was made by the *nation*, to resist the *usurpation*, and set the tyrant's *habitation* in a state of *conflagration!* which was instantly done without *hesitation*, the sword and the pistol made great *devastation*. The usurper was slain, and all of his relations followed the *liberation* of the brave *deputation*. I assure you, ladies and *gemmen*, or performers are of the first *reputation*, they use their endeavors to gain *approbation;* and the piece is adorned with superb *decoration*, so this is the booth for *gratification*.' — 'Shew 'em up, shew 'em up here, now's your time, ladies and *gemmen*, to see that extraordinary and *vonderful voman*, that never was seen before, won't be seen again, and never will be seen at all if she's not seen now. Her name is Miss Sally *Maunder*, she walks barefoot upon red hot iron, without scorching her toes, chews boiling hot lead without affecting her gums, and drinks *aqua fifties* for her beverage without giving her the belly ache.' — 'Law, bless me, Mistress Hobble Gobble, what an extraordinary vonderful voman [sic].' — 'Yes, she is, indeed, you may well says [sic] so; I can't think for the life o' me how she does it; for, here, the other night, I got rather *groggy*, and went [sic] to sleep with my *vife*, and let some hot *bacca* drop out of my pipe, and, egad, it burnt a hole in my breeches, I'm d—'d [damned] if it didn't. For my part, I can't help thinking that *she's* the devil *himself;* for, I understand as how when he does come down upon earth he always comes in the shape of a voman.' — 'Oh! for shame, for shame, you *barbarous barber*, I'll knock you down with my patten,[69] I will, you wretch! I was born to defend my sex, and I'll tell your wife of you, I will, you *waggabon*.'

Hey down, &c.
The beast with hungry tooth,

Attacks the actor's booth;
Away, affrighted run,
Priests and virgins of the sun.

1829, 1830

Charles Mathews battened on his "Humours of Bartholomew Fair," here revised as "to a country fair." He apparently freshened the cante-fable with new material, as in this printing twenty years after it was first introduced.[75]

> Spoken.] Walk up, walk up, and see the wonderful Anarabaracabaradaliana, the great Physioner from Bengal in the *Vest Hingus*; he possesses the most unparalleled, inestimable, and never-to-be-matched medicines; and can cure anything incident to humanity from a *corn* up to *consumption!* we have a long list of cures performed by his grand eliptical, Asiatical, panticarical, nervius cordial, but will only read you three out of three-thousand, the whole of which it would be tedious to read to you — this is one: — "Sir, I was cut in half in a saw pit, cured with *one* bottle." — "Sir, I was jammed to death in a linseed oil mill, cured with *two* bottles." Now comes the most wonderful of all: — "Sir, venturing too near the powder mills at Faversham, I was, by a sudden explosion, blown into a million atoms; by this unpleasant I was rendered unfit for my business (a banker's clerk), but hearing of your grand eliptical, Asiatical, panticurical, nervius cordial, I was persuaded to make essay thereof, the first bottle united my strayed particles, the second animated my shattered frame, the third effected a radical cure, the fourth sent me home to Lombard-street, to count sovereigns, carry out bills of acceptance, and recount the wonderful effect of your grand eliptical, Asiatical, panticurical nervius cordial, that cures all diseases incident to humanity." — Twenty-four ballads for a *half*penny, four and twenty for a *harf*penny consisting of the following: "Within a Mile of Edinburgh;" "Drops of Brandy;" "Cast thine eyes, my love, around;" "The Old Commodore;" "*Gin* a body meet a body;" with "London now is out of town;" sung by me and my partner"; "Strike up Poll, and tip 'em the curl." *(Sings first verse of "London Now, &c.)....*

Those in fairs who take delight,
In shows, and seeing every sight,

Dancing, singing and a fight,
    At a Country fair.
Boys by mamma's treacle fed,
With cakes and spicy gingerbread,
On every body's toes they tread,
    All at a Country fair.
Monkeys mounting camels' backs,
For prizes there men jump in sacks,
And others drinking quarts of max,[62]
    And think that that's your sort.
Corks are drawing, glasses jingle,
Trumpets, drums together mingle,
Till your heads completely tingle,
    Which quite completes the sport.

1825

Various menageries are competing for public favor at the fair.

1827

"Humours of Bartholomew Fair" is printed but without credit to Mr. Matthews. (This is still Roud ID number B41435 though greatly expanded.)

Come bustle neighbour Prig
Buckle on your flaxen wig;
In our Sunday clothes so gaily,
We'll strut up the Old Bailey;
O the devil take the rain,
We may never go again,
See the shows have begun, oh rare oh!
    Springing rattle,
    Horned cattle,
    Hot spice,
    All so nice,
    Fat ox,
    Pit and box,
    Eating fire,
    Slack wire,
    Tumble in,
    Just begin, [sic]

Spoken.] — 'Valk up, valk up, ladies and *gemmen*, here's the most wonderful birds, wild *beastes and beastesses,* there ever was seen in the vorld, or any where else alive; and just arrived from *Benegal,* in the *Vest Indies.* Here is the wonderful sea cow that can't live in the water, and dies on the land, *to be seen alive.* Only look, marm, at this *ere butiful* hanimal, no less than two hundred spots on his body, no two alike, and *every von different*; it's out of the power of any *limmer* to describe him.' — 'Vell! positively, I never *saw'd* such a *bootiful* creatur [sic] in all my born days, positively, did you, sir?' — 'A d—d fine looking animal, 'pon my word, mem.' — 'I say, Master Showman, how long do you suppose this *ere* creature is?' — 'How long! Measures fifteen feet from the tail to the snout, and twelve feet from the snout to the tail; lives! oh dam'me, lives to the *hadvanced* age of *vone hundred ears* [sic]; grows an inch and a half every *hannual year,* and never comes up to his proper growth.' — 'Stir him up, stir him up, there, keeper, with a long pole.' — 'Oh law! pa, I is so very frightened; only hear how the *vild beastesses* roars; Oh, pray do take me out, daddy, or I shall be sick. Oh la! I thinks I feels one of the tame leopards *nawing* [sic] my shoulder and shin bones.' — 'Well, you shouldn't ha'e come.' — 'Oh! then let me get under the tail of your coat.' — 'There's the wonderful and surprising sun eagle, ladies and *gemmen*; the *hotterer* the sun is, the higher he flies; and *vone* day, the sun being *hotterer* than common, he *flied higherer* than usual, and burnt one of his left wings; and though it has never burnt before[,] it has always been burnt since.

Hey down, ho down, derry derry down,
What wonders at Bartlemy Fair, O!
Come, bustle Mister Dip
Take care of Mister Snip;
Aye[,] neighbours never fear,
Come along my pretty dear;
That there's Master Saunders,
That's the little Dwarf from Flanders,
Stand aside and let's have a stare O.
    Fine toys,
    Roaring boys,
    Learned pig,
    Where's my wig?

All hit,
Higher trot,
Cups and balls,
Wooden walls,
Lollipops,
Shilling drops....

1829

Charles Mathews battened on his "Humours of Bartholomew Fair," here revised as "to a country fair." He apparently freshened the cante-fable with new material, as in this printing twenty years after it was first introduced.[75]

> Spoken.] Walk up, walk up, and see the wonderful Anarabaracabaradaliana, the great Physioner from Bengal in the *Vest Hingus*; he possesses the most unparalleled, inestimable, and never-to-be-matched medicines; and can cure anything incident to humanity from a *corn* up to *consumption!* we have a long list of cures performed by his grand eliptical, Asiatical, panticarical, nervius cordial, but will only read you three out of three-thousand, the whole of which it would be tedious to read to you — this is one: — "Sir, I was cut in half in a saw pit, cured with *one* bottle." — "Sir, I was jammed to death in a linseed oil mill, cured with *two* bottles." Now comes the most wonderful of all: — "Sir, venturing too near the powder mills at Faversham, I was, by a sudden explosion, blown into a million atoms; by this unpleasant I was rendered unfit for my business (a banker's clerk), but hearing of your grand eliptical, Asiatical, panticurical, nervius cordial, I was persuaded to make essay thereof, the first bottle united my strayed particles, the second animated my shattered frame, the third effected a radical cure, the fourth sent me home to Lombard-street, to count sovereigns, carry out bills of acceptance, and recount the wonderful effect of your grand eliptical, Asiatical, panticurical nervius cordial, that cures all diseases incident to humanity." — Twenty-four ballads for a *half*penny, four and twenty for a *harf*penny consisting of the following: "Within a Mile of Edinburgh;" "Drops of Brandy;" "Cast thine eyes, my love, around;" "The Old Commodore;" "*Gin* a body meet a body;" with "London now is out of town;" sung by me and my partner"; "Strike up Poll, and tip 'em the curl." *(Sings first verse of "London Now, &c.).*

Those in fairs who take delight,
In shows, and seeing every sight,
Dancing, singing and a fight,
    At a Country fair.
Boys by mamma's treacle fed,
With cakes and spicy gingerbread,
On every body's toes they tread,
    All at a Country fair.
Monkeys mounting camels' backs,
For prizes there men jump in sacks,
And others drinking quarts of max,
    And think that that's your sort.
Corks are drawing, glasses jingle,
Trumpets, drums together mingle,
Till your heads completely tingle,
    Which quite completes the sport.

Spoken:] Walk up, walk up, here is the Emperor of all the Conjurors, and Prince Regent of Houximepoksimehocopocococo, he shall take a red hot poker and thrust it into a barrel of gunpowder, and it will not go off; he will then load a blunderbuss with some of the *dentical* [sic] powder as would not explode, charged with twelve leaden bullets, which he will fire full in the face of any of the spectators, as pleases, without them being ever the worser, he will take the footman of any lady or gentleman and hang him up to the ceiling of the room, where he will let him hang, till he is requested by the company to let him down; he will borrow five or six shillings from any of the company, which he will never return to them, and all for his private use and emolument, without any other motive whatever. Now, my little dears, you have seen that, and the next *shall* be something else; now you have the representation of the taking of *Hallgiers*, by Lord Sir Issac Pelhoe, Esq., who was made Knight of Bath *and* Bristol for this very performance; look to the right, my little dears, and you'll see the treacherous Turks *a* loading of their guns and the poor Christian slaves a sarving out the red hot balls with their naked hands; there you see the Turkey interpreter, Salami, entreating for to go below, to save his long beard, *which* he is afraid will be shot of[f] by the cannon balls; look a little further and you will see a Mussellman blown up blown up in the air into a million of anatomies; now, my little dears, look to the left and you'll see in the middle if the ocean, the mast of a three decker man of war, with three British seamen clinging to it, *for* to save their lives and to keep up the allegory of Britannia rules the waves. Ten a penny sausages, ten a penny sassages. Bless me, they smell very nice, and look very nice, don't they. Yes, I never eat any, but I should like [—] I am not hungry now — thought what you are made of, Mr. Doleful. I don't know, I have often meant to taste them myself, but never had the *risolution* to try one of 'em, there's a sort of prejudice, I've heard some people say, they're made of — but I never mention it unless I'm certain, though it's a curious coincidence, I lost my dog Pincher on this very spot last week. Ladies and gentlemen, walk up, and see the most surprise appearance in the whole fair, by the three brothers[,] Hali, Muley, and Hassan, from the Caribbee Islands, of which I am a native myself; Hali will take a lighted torch in his hand, and jump down the throat of his brother, Muley, who will in his turn jump down the throat of his brother Hassan, and though Hassan the elder, is encumbered with the weight of his two brothers Halu and Muley, he will take another torch, throw a flip flap and jump down his own throat, leaving the spectators completely in the dark.

Yes, I own 'tis my, &c.

1830

Mathews parodied himself with yet another "The Humours of a Country Fair." That cante-fable begins:

Yes, I own 'tis my delight,
To see the laughter and the fright.
In such a motley, merry sight,
    As a country fair.
Full of riot, fun, and noise,
Little girls and ragged boys,
The very flower of rural joys,
    Is fun beyond compare.
Some are playing single-stick,
Boys in roundabouts so thick,
Maidens swinging till they're sick,
    All at a country fair.

Wooden toys and lollipops,
Ribbons, lace, and shilling hops,
Peg, and whip, and humming tops,
   At a country fair.

Spoken.] Here we are, all going to the fair in Mr. Creepy's cart! Here we are! Four and twenty of us at sixpence a-piece. I say, that's a good deal of money though, ain't it? Etc.

1831

Version(s) of the Matthews cante-fable entered oral tradition as reported by A. Hood in his novel, *"Dickey Barrett: with his ancient mariners and much more ancient cannon!"*

"Jack Love, the carpenter, timeously [sic] broke the brief temporary suspension by singing, at the full stretch of his well-modulated voice, the old English comic song of 'The humors of Bartholomew Fair,' which all either understood, or, however obfuscated, pretended so to do, as, after every chorus, which the whalers in full choir boisterously took part, the cheering and the laughter from every direction were — well, simply deafening."[76]

1839

Issac Van Amburgh is born in Fishkill, New York, in 1808. He left home at age nineteen, eventually to become associated with the menagerie of Raymond and Company, then the largest such collection of animals in captivity. Apparently, it was with this company that he acquired the knack of animal training.[77]

Van Amburgh's was the first "cat act" in a circus or menagerie. Dressed as a Roman gladiator in toga and sandals, he initially stepped into a cage with a lion, a leopard, a tiger and a panther in 1833.

A born showman, Van Amburgh was the first animal trainer to put his head into the mouth of a lion. While performing at the Richmond Hill Theatre in New York City, that feat of daring-do excited no little clamor from pulpit, press and public figures demanding he forebear. Nothing daunted, he then offered to drive a chariot pulled by lions and tigers up New York City's Broadway; his offer was declined.[78]

On occasion he would also take a child from the audience into the cage with him. A favorite Van Amburgh stunt was to act out scenes from the Bible, most notably by having a lion lie down with a lamb. And all the while, his fifty advance men slapped up posters on available walls and placed advertisements in local newspapers to announce the imminent arrival of the "unrivaled Conqueror and Manager of the whole Brute Creation."

"The greatest animal trainer of his day," to quote Charlie Griffith[79], Van Amburgh toured widely in the United States. He first toured Europe at least by January 29, 1839, when he gave a command performance at the behest of Queen Victoria at the Drury Lane Theatre.

Significantly, the queen commissioned Sir Edwin Henry Landseer to paint a portrait of "Isaac Van Amburgh and his Animals." That painting is now in the Royal Collection, Windsor. It shows Van Amburgh surrounded by a lion, tiger, leopard and panther, with a lamb on his lap.

From at least April through September, 1839, Van Amburgh, his "new trained lions" and his elephant were in London, appearing at Astley's Royal Ampitheatre, apparently with other acts including equestrians and various spectacles.

Van Amburgh's show was to tour in Europe until 1849. (A second company meanwhile may have toured the United States.) He died on November 29, 1865, in Philadelphia, to be succeeded by his son Christopher, who was still touring after the turn of the century. A daughter, who apparently took up the family business, was mauled to death in 1883 in London.[80]

Apparently Van Amburgh was a familiar enough figure to have his name, or some variation thereof attached to other songs. Vance Randolph's *Ozark Folksongs* has "The Hamburger Fair."[81]

I went to the hamburger fair,
The birds and the beasts were there.
The old raccoon, by the light of the moon,
Was combing his auburn hair.
The monkey he got drunk,
The elephant sneezed and fell on his knees,
And what became of the monk?

The first line usually reads "I went to the animal fair."

1840

"The earliest polite-text-prose version is identical to that in John Ashton's *Modern Street Ballads* (1888), except that he [Ashton] expurgates the words 'damme' and 'damned' throughout from the original appearance in *The Fountain of Mirth*...." Once more, it is Matthews revisited.[82]

Humours of Bartelmy Fair

Come bustle, neighbour Sprig, clap on your hat and wig,
In our Sunday clothes so gaily, let us strut up the Old Bailey,
O the devil take the rain, we may never go again,
See the shows have begun, O rare O!
Remember, Mr. Snip, to take care of Mrs. Snip,
There's a little boy from Flanders, and that 'ere's Master Glanders,
Stand aside, and we'll have a stare, O!
    How full's the fair, Lord Mayor,
    All is flurry, hurry, skurry [sic],
    Girls squalling, showmen bawling,
    Cats throwing, trumpets blowing,
    Rattles springing, monkeys grinning,
    Rope dancing, horses prancing,
    Sausage frying, children crying,
    Dogs of knowledge, come from College [sic]
    Slack wire, eating fire,
    Learned pigs of pigmy size,
    Funny clowns, ups and downs,
    Round about, all out,
    What a throng, all along,
    Politi's show, all the go,
    Just in time, that is prime,
    To enjoy all the fun of the fair, O!

(Spoken) Vaulk up, ladies and gentlemen, here the vonderful birds and beastesses, just arrived from Bengal in the Vest Indies. Vhy, look marm, at this here beautiful hanimal; no less than 200 spots on his belly, but no two alike and every vone different; it's out of the power of any body to describe him. Well, positively, I never saw such a beautiful creature in my life. Did you, Sir? A very fine looking animal, 'pon my soul, mem. Master Showman, how long do you suppose he measures? Vhy! Fifteen feet from the snout to the tail, and only twelve feet from the tail to the snout. He lives to the advanced age of one hundred years, grows an inch and a 'arf every hannual year, and never comes to his full growth. Stir him up with the long pole, keeper — only hear how he growls.

Here — here — the only booth in the fair for the greatest curiosity in all the known worl' — the wonderful and surprising Hottentot Venus is here, who measures three years and three quarters round her.

(Spoken) Here, here, show 'em up here, show him up here. Now's your time, Ladies and Gentlemen — only twopence each, to see that surprising Conjuror, the emperor of all conjurors, who will forfeit the enormous sum of one hundred pounds to anyone who shall perform the said wonders. Yes, ladies and gentlemen, I am no common sleight of hand man. The common sleight of hand man, they turn the things up their sleeves, and make you believe their fingers deceive your eyes. Now[,] Sir, you shall draw one card, two cards, three cards, four cards, half a dozen cards: you look on the card this side, you look on the card that side, and I say blow, by the abominable-ba-be-bo-fe-jacko-oh-fethi-swiftly-begone-quick-presto-passo-largo-mento-hi-cocco-lorum, the card is flown. Where has it gone to? That is the question. Be so kind, Sir, as to stop that young woman from getting out of the crowd; I suppose she has got it under her garter. Come, come, young woman, bring it forward, and let me hold it up, that all the company may have a squint at it.

Bow-wow, what a row
Is kicked up in Bartelmy fair, O!

Now the beasts with angry tooth all attack the booth,
Away affrighted run, birds and eagles of the sun,
Down tumbled trot legg'd Molly, who tips him the hue [blue?] hollow,
Poor Card is in the mud, O, rare, O.

(Spoken) Here, here, vaulk up, ladies and gentlemen, here's the winderful [sic] Kangaroo, just arrived from Bottomless Bay. Here us the wonderful large baboon, that danced a padolo,[83] and played at leap-frog with the celebrated Master Barinter. Here is the leopard-spotted tom cat, of the male species, which can as well see in the dark as without light. Here is the wonderful little marmoza [marmoset?] monkey, just arrived from the Isle of Liliput: hold him up to the company, master keeper. O dear me, what a little beauty, to be sure, do let me stroke the dear little creature — la! how prodigious tame he is. Yes, marm, he's always very tame to the ladies. Ye up, guvnor, what's the name of that large bird there, stuck up in the corner? Vat! that there vone? Oh! that's the wonderful Sun eagle, the hotter the sun is, the higher he flies. There's the wonderful Cow, that can't live on dry land, and dies in the water. Billy, Billy, my boy, go and stuff a blanket in that ['] ere hole, or the little ones vill peep for nothing, Here, here, now's your time, ladies and gentlemen, jest a going to begin, jest a going to begin. Stand off the steps there, you boys, and make way for that gentleman with the smock frock and carbuncled nose to come down. How did you like it, Sir? Oh, it's all dam stuff. There, there, only hear what a good character the gentleman gives it. Vaulk up, ladies and gemmen, now's your time to see that wonderful wooden Roscius, Mr. Punch, for the small charge of vone penny. Show your tricks, Mr. Punch.

1854

The Hannibal, Mo., *Tri-Weekly Advertiser* of August 22, 1854, carried an advertisement for Van Amburgh's Menagerie coming to town.[84]

1855

The lord mayor proclaims Bartholomew Fair for the last time in 1855.[85]

1859

Van Amburgh and Company are touring in rural Mississippi.[86]

1862

This is the first of three reprints — all without credit to Dr. Wetmore — that suggest the assumed publication date of Wetmore's song of 1865 is incorrect. (See below.) It is printed in "Bob Hart's Plantation Songster":

Vanamburgh's Menagerie[87]

Old Vanamburgh is the man that runs all these [']ere shows,
He goes into the lion's den and shows you all he knows,
He sticks his head in the lion's mouth and holds it there a while,
Then he pulls it out again and turns around and smiles.

Chorus:
The elephant now moves round, the music begins to play,
Them boys around the monkeys' cage had better keep away.

The first is the African polar bear, oft called the iceberg's daughter,
Has been known to eat six tons of ice and call for soger water.
He wades in the river up to his knees, not fearing any harm,
You may growl and snarl all you please, but he don't care a darn.

The hyena in the next cage, most wonderful to relate,
Got awful hungry the other night and ate up his female mate.
Don't go near his cage; he will hurt you little boys,
For when he's mad, he wags his tail and makes an awful noise.

The next is the anaconda boa-constrictor, called the anasabrunity,
He can eat up a toad or an elephant and is noted for his great longility;
He can swallow his head, crawl through himself, come out with great facility,
And tie himself in a big bow-knot and wink with great agility.

The monkey in the next cage is cuffing his little brother,
He's not to blame for doing that, for he learned it of his mother.
The skin of his face is drawn so tight, and covered all over with marks,
That when he winks, he's sure to gape, and when he gapes, he winks.

The last is the eagle, awful bird from the highest mountain tops,
Has been known to eat up little birds and here his history stops;
The performance can't go on, there is too much noise and confusion,
If the ladies give them monkeys fruit, it will injure their constitution.

1862

The folk tradition is already at work. The *Yale Literary Magazine* has this facetious editor's note:[88]

The sleepy editor is awakened by 'the psalm tune Van Amburgh' [cast] in a merry old walk-around, singing the whole while:

"Next comes the animaconda boa's constrictor, called animaconda for brevity, Who can swallow an elephant as well as a toad and is noted for his longevity, He'll swallow himself, crawl through himself, come out with great facility, Then tie himself, in a bow-knot, snap his tail and wink with agility.

"He [the editor] has done his task and the Lit. is ready for the printer. Therefore he joins the mighty 'chorious' and willingly proclaims that, 'The elephant now goes round and the band begins to play, And the boys around the monkey's cage had better keep away.'

1865 [?]

The dubious date of this sheet music was assigned by the Levy Collection in the Johns Hopkins Library Collection. (The cover of the sheet music has a typo; there is no apostrophe after the letter H.) The title thus reads "Van Amburghs [sic] Menagerie/ A Comic Song by Dr. W.J. Wetmore." The first page of the sheet music corrects the typo, and credits W.J. Wetmore, M.D.

Van Amburgh's Menagerie[89]

Old Van Am-burgh is the man that runs all these 'ere shows; He goes in-to the li-on's den and shows you all he knows; He sticks his head in the li-on's mouth and holds it there a-while; Then he pulls it out a-gain and turns a-round and smiles. The e-le-phant now moves 'round, the mu-sic be-gins to play; the

boys a-round the mon-key's cage had bet-ter keep a-way.

Old Van Amburgh is the man that runs all these ere [sic] shows,
He goes into the lion's den and shows you all he knows.
He sticks his head in the lion's mouth and holds it there a while,
Then he pulls it out again and turns around andsmiles.

CHORUS:
The elephant now moves round. The music begins to play.
Them boys around the monkey's cage had better keep away.

There's the polar bear we sometimes call the iceberg's daughter,
He'll eat six tons of ice a day, and frolics in the water,
He wades the deepest rivers, which scarcely wet his knees,
And he never catches cold, for you never hear him sneeze.

The peacock is a pretty bird, his tail is wondrous fine,
The jaybird and the jackdaw are mad to see it shine.
The kangaroos are jumping, and rattling the cage door,
Look out, you little boys, for the lion's going to roar.

The monkey in the next cage is cuffing his little brother.
He's not to blame for doing that for he learned it of his mother;
The skin of his face is drawn so tight, and covered o'er with kinks,
That when he winks, he's sure to gape, and when he gapes, he winks.

The last is the eagle, from the highest mountain tops,
He's known to eat up little birds, and here his history stops;
The performance can't go on, there is too much noise and confusion,
If the ladies give them monkeys fruit, it will injure their constitution.

The Wetmore composition also entered oral tradition; it too shows signs of "folk re-creation."
The first verse runs:

Van Amberg is the man who owns all of the shows[,]
Goes into the lion's den and shows you all he knows[,]
Puts his head in the lion's mouth, holds it there a while[,]
When he takes it out, he makes all the people smile.

Chorus:
The elephant now is movin' round, the band begins to play.
Boys around the monkeys' cage had better keep away.

The bald-headed eagle's in the first cage, from farmost mountain tops,
Known to eat up little boys and then he'd lick his chops;

The kangaroo is jumpin' 'round and shakin' this cage door.
Look out, ya little fella for the lion is goin' to roar.[90]

1866

"Selected Songs Sung at Harvard College from 1862 to 1866" contains a hand-written inscription dated "June 1866."

Menagerie Song[91]

Van Amburg is the man that goes with all the shows;
He goes into the lions' den, and shows you all he knows.
He sticks his head in the lion's mouth, and keeps it there awhile;
And, when he takes it out again, he greets you with a smile.

Chorus:
For the elephant now goes round;
The band begins to play:
Those boys around the monkeys' cage,
They'd better keep away.

This is the Arctic polar bear, oft called the iceberg's daughter:
Been known to eat three tubs of ice, then call for soda-water;
She wades in the water up to her knees, not fearing any harm;
You may growl and grumble as much as you please, but she don't care a darn.

Next comes the baboon Emmeline, catching flies and scratching her head;
Weeping and wailing all the day, because her husband's dead,
Poor weeping, wailing water-lily, of all her friends bereft;
That monkey is thumbing his nose at her, with his right paw over his left.[92]

Next comes the anaconda-boa-constrictor, called the anaconda for brevity;
He can swallow an elephant as well as a toad, and is noted for his great longevity;
Can swallow himself, crawl through himself, come out with great facility,
Tie himself in a bow-knot, snap his tail, and wink with great agility.

That hyena in the next cage, most wonderful to relate,
Got awful hungry the other night, and ate up his female mate.
Now, don't go near his cage; he'll hurt you, little boys;
For when he's mad, he'll growl and bite, and make a horrible noise.

Next comes the condor, an awful bird, from the highest mountain-tops:
Been known to eat up little boys, and then to smack his chops.
This performance can't go on; there's too much noise and confusion:
Those ladies giving those monkeys nuts will injure their constitution.

1867

Doctor Wetmore's song was obviously popular on college campuses.[93] The song is now entitled "Menagerie" and Wetmore is uncredited. The five verses run:

Van Amburgh is the man, who goes to all the shows,
He goes into the lion's den, and tells you all he knows;
He sticks his head in the lion's mouth, And [sic] keeps it there a while,
And when he takes it out again, he greets you with a smile.

CHORUS:
The elephant goes round, the band begins to play,
The boys around the monkey's cage had better keep away.

First comes the African Polar Bear, oft called the iceberg's daughter,
She's been known to eat three tubs of ice, then call for soda water;
She wades in the water up to her knees, not fearing any harm,
And you may grumble all you please and she don't care a darn.

That hyena in the next cage, most wonderful to relate,
Got awful hungry the other day, and ate up his female mate;
He's a very ferocious beast, don't go near him, little boys,
For when he's mad he shakes his tail, and makes this awful noise.
   Imitation of growling.

Next comes the Anaconda Boa Constrictor, oft called Anaconda for brevity,
He's known the world throughout for his age and great longevity;
He can swallow himself, crawl through himself and come out again with facility,
He can tie himself up in a double-bow-knot with his tail and wink with
   the greatest agility.

Next comes the vulture, awful bird, from the mountain's highest tops,
He's been known to eat up little girls, and then to lick his chops;
Oh, the show it can't go on, there's too much noise and confusion.

1870

This is apparently unusual in that a song, "The Royal Wild Beast Show," clearly of British origin is included, unchanged, in a songster printed in New York City. It was set to music by Alfred Lee (d. 1906). Composer and sometime lyricist Lee was apparently very successful in late Victorian England, particularly when providing songs for music hall singer George Leybourne, best known for performing Lee's 1867 song "Champagne Charlie."[94]

The Royal Wild Beast Show[95]

Come stand aside, good people all, and hear what I've to say,
But let the little dears come up, what's going for to pay.
At all the courts in Europe we are reckon'd quite the go,
Then pay your sixpences and see the Royal Wild Beast Show.

CHORUS:
The camomiles, the crocodiles, and all that you could wish;
The mice and rats, and tabby cats, and other kinds of fish;
A dozen sphinxes upside down, and standing in a row,
It's only sixpence each to see the Royal Wild Beast Show.

The first one is the kangaroo, you'll know him by his hump;
The next's the hippopotamus, you ought to see him jump.
The third's the alligator and he's such a one to crow,
He wakes us every morning in the Royal Wild Beast Show.

That pretty thing's the oozley bird, the other one's his aunt,
The third we call the pelican, the next the peli*cant;*
The other one's the solon [sic, for salon] goose — you musn't call out bo!
Or you will hurt his feelings in the Royal Wild Beast Show.

The donkey in the corner with the tiger on his arm,
Comes from *Ass*yria, where once his father kept a farm;
The billy goat that's dressed in pink and walking rather slow,
Is very *horn*imental in a Royal Wild Beast Show.

The tortoise, famous for his speed, unequal'd by a horse;
The parrot, too, who talks in *polly*-syllables, of course;
The raging elephants that roar when stormy winds do blow,
Are also represented in the Royal Wild Beast Show.

The next one is a mighty ape, indeed, I tell you true,
It's only natural he should "go walking in the Zoo;"
Our stock of monkeys, you'll observe, at present is but low —
They are so plentiful outside the Royal Wild Beast Show.

The last's the boa-constrictor, who eats all he finds about —
Why, who's been fool enough to let the nasty crittur [sic] out?
He's somewhere underneath the chairs, hi! mind your legs, hullo!
He's very quick in clearing out the Royal Wild Beast Show.

1876

The folk process churns up a fusion of three separate songs in this text reprinted "by permission of the author, C.T. Miller, of Providence, R.I."[96]

The Menagerie

Come all and listen to me, and as you stand around,
I will show you the greatest menagerie that ever was in town.
We are here in a great cloth tent with cages round the sides.
There is the elephant Emeline over there that everybody rides.

Von Humbug is the man that owns all these [']ere shows.
He'll get into the lion's den ami [sic, for and] shows you all he knows.
He'll put his head in the lion's mouth, and hold it there a while.
He'll take it out again pretty soon, and then look around and smile.

That leopards never change their spots he'll prove to be a blunder.
He'll make them lay in this 'ere spot, then change to that spot yonder.
He moves among the savage brutes, not fearing any harm.
They may growl and snarl all they please but he don't care a cent [sic, for show alarm? Give a darn?]

With the wonderful Rhino-noceros [sic], the program does begin.
He wades in water up to his knees and then wades out again.
That horn on top of his nose is a toothpick he cannot use
Except to pick up human beings and shake 'em right out of their shoes.

Here's the giraffe-camel-leopard with a great long spotted throat,
His head's so high and out of town, that he ain't allowed to vote.
With forelegs long and hind legs short, he scampers o'er the plain.
And his long legs often rest themselves till the short catch up again.

Here's the wonderful Dromedary, double-breasted in the back,
You see his toes are cracked in two so he always toes the crack.
When in Noah's ark, they got him mad, and drove him round and round,
And Drommy got his back up, and never got it down.

And here's the golden eagle, America's proud bird.
They say he "shouts for liberty," but he never says a word.
He puts his head beneath his wing, makes seventy-six gyrations.
Then whistles "Yankee Doodle' and shrieks the variations.

That zebra standing in the next cage there, too sleepy to kick or bite,
Has a thousand marks across his back and Harry [sic, for nary] one alike.
The skin on his face is drawn so tight, and covered up with marks,
That when he gapes, he's sure to wink, and when he winks he gapes. [sic]

The next, the African polar bear, often called the iceberg's daughter,
Has been known to eat ten tons of ice, then call for soda water.
The performance can't go on, there's too much noise and confusion.
Ladies, don't give those monkeys fruit; it will injure their constitution.

That speckled snake in the blanket there, noted for great longevity,
Is Anna Maria Condor Boa Constrictor snake, called Anaconda for brevity.
She will tie herself in thirteen knots, and eat with great voracity,
Swallow her head, turn inside out, and go backwards with great alacrity.

That kangaroo that is hopping about, and cuffing his little brother,
Is not to blame for doing so, for he learned it of his mother.
He measures eighteen feet you see, I measure with this cane [sic]
He's nine feet long from head to tail, and nine feet back again.

Now, John, stir up those monkeys, and, Jimmie, feed the bear,
Make Christopher Columbus and Washington fight, and pull one another's hair.
Here is the monkey[,] "Drooping Lily," of all her friends bereft,
The ourang outang is looking love at her, with his right hand "over the left."

Here is the Crying Hyena, of the insect tribe, most wonderful of all,
He makes night hideous and daylight too by his everlasting squall.
With tearful eyes he roams about, and snaps at all the boys,
And once in fifteen minutes makes this remarkable noise. (Yell)

The last is the vulture — awful bird — from the highest mountain tops,
He stuffs himself with little birds, and here his history stops.
The audience will please retire. The hyena is getting mad.
The boys have got the monkeys cross, and Emeline is feeling bad.

1878

This is the first report of the "raree show." The purported author of this parlor-presentable variant is James Burdette. His "The Irishman's Panorama" does contain the command: "James, move the crank! Larry, music on the bagpipes!" Four more times, the narrator commands: "Move the crank, etc."[97]

1880s

William C. Smith reminisced in *Queen City Yesterdays: Sketches of Cincinnati in the Eighties* his memories of a misspent youth:

"…His spiel was often parodied by the more sophisticated of that generation and such parodies in time trickled down to the lower age levels and provided amusement for youths of the mature age of thirteen. It is regrettable that such parodies cannot be reprinted…."[98]

1884

This is again "James S. Burdette's Irishman's Panorama," non-bawdy parody in the spirit of the raree show with at least one instance of "James, move the crank! Larry, music on the bagpipes!"[99]

1887

William F. Cody brings his Wild West Show to London for the first time, the Queen requesting a command performance. The Cody troupe is a great success.

1888

Gershon Legman has dated this variant, published in "The Stag Party," to 1888 because of a reference to the presidential campaign of that year. Given its frequent references, however, to the California Gold Rush of 1848–1855, a possible date for the creation of the "raree show" tradition might be approximately 1854. The City and County of San Francisco passed a law restricting the immigration of Chinese women within the city limits. (By 1860, an estimated 85 percent of all Chinese women worked as prostitutes.)

Before the turn of the century, magic lantern had replaced panoramas. For example, shows in Cincinnati "were often presented one of the Halls of the West End. In these professional productions, geographical, historical and other scenes were shown. Such exhibits were advertised by a barker who assumed the title 'professor.' He stood next to a cloth screen and after rattling off each description would call out, 'Larry, turn the crank,' when his assistant would run in another slide."[100]

Three copies of "The Stag Party" are known to exist, according to Legman; this is taken from the library of the Kinsey Institute, Indiana University. It is presented here verbatim.

SHORT SKETCHES OF BIBLE HISTORY.

A story is told of an Irishman who had been mining with very little success in California and to whom a Yankee had sold a "Peep Show" with which he had been raking in the shekels to a great extent for some time previous. The first arrangement was that the vendor should accompany the Irishman and do the lecturing part of the show at so much a week; but at the end of the first week Pat thought he had mastered the set speeches which the Yankee invariably used sufficiently to dispense with his services and by doing the talking himself could save about twenty dollars a week. He accordingly started out with only a small boy to turn the crank, and had no sooner put up the Peep Box than a big six-foot ten-inch miner presented himself and forked out the fifty cents for a peep at the panorama.

"Now," says Pat, "ye just put your eye against the hole and keep it there until you hear me say, 'boy turn the crank,' and then look what you'll see. You're ready, are you?" "Yes." "Then boy turn the crank and there you see the Garden of Eden, the garden itself can easily be distinguished by the beautiful flowers you see all around and the little birds singing on the branches of the trees and all as tame as barn-door chickens. That's Eve over there, the beautiful naked woman with a fig-leaf over her twot; and the fine looking young man standing beside her feeling her bubbies that's Adam. All he's got on, too, is a fig-leaf, and that aint big enough to hide his damned old dingus, for you see the head and neck of it hanging down perceptibly, while his balls are exposed entirely. But you mustn't look too long. Boy, turn the crank. And that shows you Daniel in the lion's den. There's no use pointing Dan out, because he's the only man there, nor the lion, that big ferocious baste you see in the corner snapping and grabbing all the time at the prophet's bare arse; but there's one that that can't be pointed out, for neither you nor I nor any one else can see him, and that's the angel of the Lord who stands by unbeknown'st to them all and hinders the lion each bite he makes. But the prophet, you see, feels that the angel is there, though he can't see him, and that's why he turns his arse to the lion with scornful in difference. So much for having faith in the Lord. Boy, turn the crank.

"Now you have the third scene. That's the Deluge, when, as the good book says, 'the waters covered the whole face of the earth; and the Ark of Noah floated about upon the waters.' There's the ark on the great waste waters, as you will notice, and not a single sign of land as far as the eye can reach; you see the three men sitting on deck enjoying the beautiful sunset and their evening cigar, that's Noah and his two sons, Shem and Japhet. You can't see Ham for he's down in the hold shoveling shit from the animals' quarters, and it's all the black son-of-a bitch is good for anyway. Boy, turn the crank.

57

"And here you see Balaam on his way to curse the children of Israel. But the children of Israel, you know, are the chosen people of God, so when Balaam is on his way he is stopped by an angel, who warns him to go back at once and that he'd be wise to hold his jaw and not say another word. 'Sure it was my ass spoke, not me,' says the prophet. 'So I should judge from the smell,' says the angel, 'and you ought to be ashamed to behave so before the angel of the Lord,' on which it disappeared and Balaam turned back overwhelmed with the rebuke. Boy, turn the crank.

"And this gives the fifth scene — Lot and his two daughters. You'll observe there's only one of the girls there, the other is waiting outside the cave while the ould man puts the blocks to her sister. It's not the right thing to do, I know, being contrary to the laws of God and man, but they seem to be liking it anyway, and maybe we shouldn't be too hard on them as they all think they're the only ones left on the face of the earth, and that it's their duty to do all they can to re-people it; and, besides that, I'm thinking the morals of none of them is the best, for you know they had been living for years in Sodom, and Sodom, we know, was the worst place for wild fucking of all descriptions that's mentioned in the bible (barring Chicago). Boy, turn the crank.

"Now this gives us another fucking scene, leastways it is not exactly a fucking scene, though it came near being one. It shows you Joseph and Potiphar's wife. Now Mrs. Potiphar you'll know was the most beautiful woman at the court of Pharoah, but she was an arrant whore and had set her heart on having a piece from Joseph, who was a comely lad in the full vigor of youth. But then, you see, Joseph was a high-principled young fellow and he tells Mrs. Potiphar that he never could reconcile it with his conscience to make so free with his master's wife, for she had just been asking him to go upstairs and have one of them[?] things; but no, he would rather risk being sent to a loathsome dungeon than accede to her solicitations, which shows the difference between him and you, you son-of-a-bitch, who would give up your last five dollar piece to have a rap at the damndest old Chinese whore that ever came prowling about the diggings."

"Who are you calling a son-of-a-bitch?" asks the man at the peep hole, "I'm calling you a son-of-a-bitch," says Pat, and with that the audience jumps up and lets Pat have one under the ear, and Pat returns on the other's nose, and there they grapple and fall over carrying the Peep Show with them and smashing it all to pieces, and in less than two minutes we have them both rolling about in the mud chewing each other's ears and noses to their heart's content.

ca. 1890s

Performed by Willy Smith, the text is attributed to James White. Again this is a bawdy recitation, accompanied by a harmonica.[101] The compressed narrative begins with the first panel of the spooled pictures, wanders off to deal with the bawdy recitation "Daniel in the Lion's Den," and ends ultimately with the narrator offering to fight anyone who calls him a fakir [sic].

"Michael Casey Exhibiting His Panorama,"
a humorous selection by Willy Smith.

ANNOUNCER: Ladies and gentlemen, I take pleasure tonight in introducing to you Mister — Mister Michael Jeremiah Casey, the great American explorer from New York City. He has tonight that he's going to show to you their panny-murra, pa-, panny-ma, panny...

CASEY: Aw, sit down, you're making a bollocks of the whole damn business, what the hell's the matter with you, sit down. Gentlemen, I'll introduce myself. Now I have tonight that I'm going to show to you a panorama and I hope that you will all be pleased with the pictures and if you don't, well, I don't give a shit anyhow, turn the crank there. [Music played on harmonica] Turn back, turn back, God damn it. [More music] There. Gentlemen, this is the first picture. Faith, Hope — and Charity. I'll ask you to notice the titties on Hope and the arse on Faith and the snatch on Charity. It is rumored that Hope took it in the pooper, that is the cause of her wide arse, turn the crank there, turn it. [Music played on harmonica] Wait, wait. [More music] Turn back, God damn it, you'll break that machine. Turn back!

There. Gentlemen, this is the next picture. Daniel in the lion's den. You know that Daniel was thrown in the lion's den by the King of Ireland, and the king's name was Brown, and he had a very beautiful daughter named Brown, and Daniel being very fond of Brown and thought she'd make good brown and tried to get up her brown. Well, anyhow, the King thrown him in and one day he comes along and says, "Hey, hello, Daniel, you're in the hole." "What hole," says Daniel. "Arse hole," says the King. "Kiss it," says Daniel, which shows that Daniel was full of repartee.

Ow, turn the crank, turn her away there. [Music played on harmonica] Wait, wait, what the hell's the matter with you, God damn it, wait.

Here — gentlemen, here's the next picture. This is Venus. You know a Venus was a cousin to a Penis, and one night when Venus was way in … Penis out of sight, says Venus to Penis, "Sure, by God, I couldn't tell there was anything between us."

Oh, owow, turn away, turn away, turn away, run it along. [Music played on harmonica]

INTERJECTION: Say, Reilly, why the devil don't the lions bite Daniel?

CASEY: Bite your ass, God damn it, the lions have no teeth, what the hell is the matter with you, turn the crank, turn it, turn it. There, gentlemen, the next picture. This is the horse's arse. Note that the horse's arse is the east end of a cow's tits going south. And that's the kind of a man I am.

INTERJECTION: Ah, you're a fakir, Reilly, you're a fakir.

CASEY: Who's a fakir, who's a fakir, I'll come down and lick that man.[101]

1908

This is the first recovered appearance of the now common chorus of "The Wild West Show," oddly enough in a college cheer.[102] However, it would seem that it was more commonly known. A Google search finds that in 1911, a University of Michigan annual quoted the line, "We're going to see the whole show through." An edition of the *San Bernardino Sun* of 1915 noted "as the old song goes, 'We're going to see the whole show through.'"

Where are we going?
Oh, we're going to the Hamburg Show,
To see the elephant and the kangaroo,
And we'll all stick together through rain and stormy weather .
For we're going to see the whole show through.

Let's try Rickety Kax, one, two, three
Ricketey Kax! Go ax, go ax,
Give them the ax, the ax, the ax.

1908

"The Hamburg Show" as presented by the Delta chapter of Sigma Nu at the University of Michigan as a benefit on May 1 and 2, 1908 "was a take-off on a one-ring circus." It opened with a Spanish Dance, followed by Nero, the human horse; successive "acts" included an elephant, a "Phoenecian wolf"; the Esau, the wild man who eats raw meat; and finally Fearless Frieda who tames Raja the tiger.

1913

Dr. Wetmore's mid-19th Century song finds yet another adaptation.

"Van Amburgh's Menagerie"[103]

"This can be made very enjoyable for a large audience."

Text begins: "Scene First":

> Band marching in, followed by elephants and showman. "Now boys, you must all clear out; this is the place for the show; Go and get your tickets."... Attendants push the crowd out, then the band begins to play; the animals pick up cages and march out; the elephant goes last; then the band, and last the showman, making elegant bows to the audience."

ca. 1914

To John Brophy and Eric Partridge go credit for the first, almost, unexpurgated text of a bawdy version of "The Wild West Show."[104] They added, "Pre-war, but made much more generally known during the Great War, was a lengthy recitation, *The Showman*, which many learned by ear or by heart. Several versions are known. This is one of the best." Significantly, this is the first recovered cross-over of the barker form into what might be called the mainstream.

> First of all, ladies and gentlemen, and I trust that you ladies will forgive my French, we have the chamois. Well, the shameless chamois jumps from precipice to precipice and back to piss again...

Ah, now the rhinoceros, the richest animal in the world, to those familiar with the Classics, the derivation of its name is interesting; *rhino*, meaning money, *soreass*, meaning piles. There you have it, ladies and gentlemen: piles of money.

And next the leopard, one spot for every day of the year. 'What about Leap Year?' Bill, just lift his tail.

This is the laughing hyena. The animal drinks once a week, eats once a month, and never has any sexual intercourse, so what he's got to laugh at I don't know!

Here is the Wild Man of Borneo. He has no cock. 'How does he — [fuck], guv'nor?' He can't; that's what makes him so bloody wild.

I will now show you the camel. This peculiar animal eats mud, shits bricks, and has a triangular arse-hole. Hence the Pyramids.

We now come to the whoo-hoo bird. He eats red pepper and flies backwards… [to cool his asshole]. Hence the trade winds.

Here we have the wagga-wagga bird, which scours the local villages in search of his prey. On finding the finest specimen of the female of his species he carries her off to his mountain lair, where he proceeds to — [fuck] her, uttering the while his plaintive cry of 'wagga-wagga'. This, being interpreted from the language of birds, signifies, 'Gawd, how lovely!'

The armoured armadillo! This is an extraordinary beast. When pursued by his foes, does he run away? No! Does he climb trees? No!! He retreats and farts defiance at his nonplussed foes.

And finally we have the oozolem foozlem bird. This bird, ladies and gentlemen, once a year descends from his mountain fastnesses into the valleys below. He then stalks through the villages till he finds the fairest and most virtuous of the opposite sex. Then he — [fucks] her, and finally eats her, thus avoiding for his unfortunate victim the shame and disgrace which would otherwise be her lot.

Now then, you small boys, get into the boats: the elephant's about to piss.

1917

Jonathan Lighter graciously pointed out that John Dos Passos in his *The Fourteenth Chronicle* included the blameless chorus in his entry for June 26, 1917. Dos Passos then was then aboard the transport S.S. Chicago on his way to volunteer as an ambulance driver.

It is worth pointing out that Dos Passos apparently learned the song in the United States, which would suggest that it was older, perhaps much older, in its ever unsettled "final" form.

> Where are we going boys?
> 'Oh, we're bound for the Hamburg show
> To see the elephant and the wild kangaroo
> And we'll all stick together
> In fair or foul weather
> For we're going to see the damn show through.'

1918

Under the headline "Band Music Cheers Soldiers at Front," the *Ashland Tidings* of June 24, 1918, ran a short story quoting the now familiar chorus:

> We're going to the Hamburg fair,
> To see the elephant and the kangaroo,
> We'll all stick together in all kinds of weather,
> For we're going to see the whole show through.

ca. 1918

"It seems that back around 1918, the little town of Hamburg had an annual circus which the University of Michigan students attended. This song was made up by the students about [the] circus. There was a never ending string of verses, which became more crude as they go along..."[105]

> CHORUS (to follow each verse):
> We're going to the Hamburg Show,
> To see the elephants and the wild kangaroos.

We'll all stick together in fair or stormy weather,
And we're going to see the whole show through.

SPOKEN:
"And in the next cage, ladies and gentlemen,
And in the next cage [sic], we have Mr. and Mrs. Carriage,
And their daughter, Miss Carriage.

"And in the next cage, ladies and gentlemen,
And in the next cage, we have the leopard
Who has a spot for every day in the year.
What's that, lady? Leap year?
Look under the tail, lady.

"And in the next cage, ladies and gentlemen,
And in the next cage, we have the ostrich.
Now the snake goes in the ostrich's mouth
And comes out of his rear,
And the ostrich put his mouth up to his rear and said,
Loop-de-loop, you son of a bitch!

"And in thus next cage, ladies and gentlemen,
And in this next cage, we have the orangoutang [sic].
He jumps from precipice to precipice and back to piss again,
He jumps from precipice to precipice and back to piss again.

CHORUS:
We're off to the hamburg show
To the elephants and wild kangaroos.
And we'll all stick together in fair and stormy weather,
And we'll all see the whole show through.

1920

Reuss cited just one stanza: "This hanimile, gents, is the laughing hyena; he's very strange, he eats only once a year, fucks once every six years, and yet — "when there came a voice from the crowd, "Then what the hell 'as he got to laugh at?" Reuss's note states, "[The] context is a story-telling session on board a shipload of modern-day pirates. The volume is a humorous fantasy: a mixture of humorous and impossible adventure with extensive — and almost impossible — sexual activity." A copy is in the Institute for Sex Research, Bloomington, Indiana.

1920

An advertisement in the June, 1920, issue of *School and Home Education:*

The Hamburg Show

Ladies and Gentlemen!!!

Oh, we're going to the Hamburg Show
To see the Elephant and the wild kangaroo!
And we'll stick together
Through rain and stormy weather
For we're going to see the whole show through!

> "The next cage, Ladies and Gentlemen, contains the Wild Man of Borneo! He's wild, and sirs, he's ferocious. Watch him as he grits his teeth and snarls his savage snarl.
> "He was not always thus. In his younger days he was in business. As the years went in, however, in his native isle the brisk competition of jungle trade slowly forced him out of business.
> "'But,' says the Lady-on-the-Front-Seat, 'how did he advertise?'
> "'Madam, he did not advertise, — that's what makes him wild...'"

Clearly, the individual who wrote this advertisement was familiar with "The Hamburg Show."

1921

Under the title, "Nonsense, Larry," the humor magazine, "Capt. Billy's Whiz Bang," printed two expurgated stanzas of the panorama or raree show variant:

> "The next picture, ladies and gentlemen, is that of the Rocky Mountain goat. You can't get this goat's goat because he leaps from precipice to precipice and back to crag again. And every time he leaps he grunts and every time he grunts he leaps.

"—Turn the crank, Larry.

"The next picture is that of the laughing hyena which is a species of animal life that made the wild cat wild. The laughing hyena eats only once a week and drinks once a year, so I don't know whyinel [why in hell] he laughs so much.

"—Turn the crank, Larry."[107]

1921

The first volume of the *McGill University Song Book* contained not only "The Menagerie" but "Hamburgh" as well. The editors were apparently unaware of the tangled history of cross-fertilization.[108]

The Hamburg Show

The Menagerie

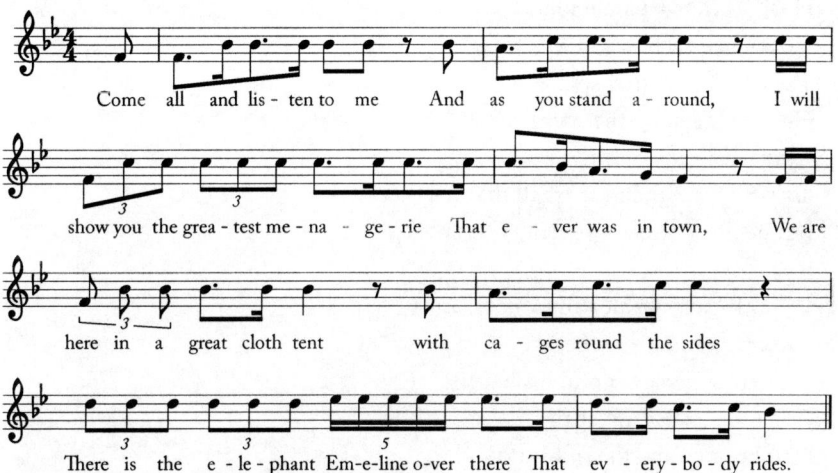

Come all and listen to me,
And as you stand around,
I will show you the greatest menagerie
That ever was in town;
We all are here in a great cloth tent,
With cages round the sides,
There is the Elephant Emeline over there,
That ev'ry body rides.

CHORUS:
The Elephant will now move round,
The music begin [sic] to play,
Those boys around the Monkeys' cage
Will please to keep away,
Will please to keep away.

Van Amburgh is the man
That owns these 'ere shows,
He'll get into the lion's den
And show you all he knows.
He'll put his head in the lion's mouth,
And hold it there a while,
He'll take it out again pretty soon,
And look around and smile. CHORUS.

That leopards never change their spots
He'll prove to be a blunder.
He'll make them lay in this 'ere spot,
Then change to that spot yonder.
He moves among the savage brutes
Not fearing any harm.
They may growl and snarl all that they please,
But he don't care a——cent. CHORUS.

With the wonderful Rhino-noceros
The programme does begin.
He wades in water up to his knees,
And then wades out again.
That horn on the top of his nose
Is a toothpick he cannot use.
Except to pick up human beings
And shake them right out of their shoes. CHORUS.

1925

Jonathan Lighter by email to Ballad-L@iulistserve.Indiana.edu, December 1, 2006, noted that in the June, 1925, issue of *The American Mercury*, gadfly critic H.L. Mencken dilated upon some failings of the "folk-lorists of the Republic."

> Most of them are schoolmarms, male or female, and their interest is concentrated on more seemly heroes and more gentle legends.... [T]hey have given little attention to the geste of Bunyan and none at all to such noble American sagas as that of Larry and the panorama. Who, having heard any part of the latter, will ever forget it? 'This strange beast, ladies and gentlemen, is the laughing hyeneus.... What's he got to laugh about, I'll be damned if I know!' And the ibex, pursuing the female of the species through the primeval forest! And the cassowary! And the astounding bird that laid the bricks for Cheops' pyramid! The epic of Larry has been reduced to paper by more than one exhilarated scribe, but I don't believe that it has ever been printed, even privately. A chance for the Yale University Press or the Carnegie Institution! Who wrote it? That is, who began to write it? No one seems to know. I have been told that Mark Twain made contributions to it. It is surely not improbable. But it was old when Mark Twain was a boy. I suspect that

scores of ingenious men have had their hands in it — that it is, more than any ballad ever heard of, a genuinely popular collaboration.

It is a pity that our national prudery prevents its publication, even for the use of the learned and the damned. It is, in parts, unquestionably loose and ribald, but there is certainly nothing disgusting in it — nothing half so disgusting, indeed, as the furtive, half-pathological indecencies that burden all the newstands and pack the Broadway show-stops. Its humors are the humors of the unfettered male, taking his ease with his kind; any man who is not moved to laughter is *ipso facto*, a Freudian case.

Lighter noted, "The version that Mencken knew was of the 'Larry, Turn the Crank,' variously printed as 'The Hamburg Show' two years later in *Immortalia*, pp. 153–54. And indication of just how widespread the recitation may have been by 1930 is that precisely *none* of the creatures Mencken enumerates appear in the *Immortalia* text of 1927."

1926

From the Canfield Manuscript, which John Patrick has dated to 1926:

"In my memory are a lot of verses to what we of Michigan called 'The Hamburg Show' in which verse follows verse retelling the same exploits, no doubt, as 'Larry and His Panorama.' I will try to write out a few which you may not have. At the conclusion of each [verse], the previous reciter would say, 'Where we going, boys?' to which the chorus made answer:

"We're going to the Hamburg Show
To see the elephant and the wild kangaroo.
And we'll all stick together
In fair or stormy weather,
For we're going to see the whole show through.

"And then the next verse would be recited by a new voice."

The letter was signed by one Lyons, who was, at the time, a member of the staff at New York's Mount Sinai Hospital.

1927

This is the melding of both the raree show and Van Amburgh variants as printed in *Immortalia* credited to "A Gentleman about Town" in a privately printed edition of 1,000 copies, "none of which were for general sale." There is a reasonable surmise that the "town" is Berkeley, California, home of the University of California, arch-rival of Stanford University. (See stanza five.) The original quadrangle at Stanford is built of irregular sandstone bricks.[110]

The Hamburg Show

Ladies and gents, are you ready? Larry, turn the crank —

CHORUS:
For we're going to see the Hamburg Show,
See the monkey and the wild kangaroo,
And we'll all stick together in all sorts of weather,
For we're gonna see the whole show through.

And in the next cage, we have the South American llama who roams the wild mountain ranges of the Andes, leaping from precipice to precipice, and back to piss again. Larry, turn the crank, etc.

And in the next cage we have the Javanese baboon who is so fat that every time he winks his eye he skins his prick. The ladies delight in throwing sand in his eyes to watch him masturbate. Larry, turn the crank.

And in the next cage we have the Australian ostrich who, when frightened, sticks his head deep down in the desert sand and farts. Hence the antipodal trade winds.

And in the next cage, we have the spotted leopard who has a spot for each day of the year. You ask, lady, what he does in leap year? Under his tail, madam, you will find the extra spot. Larry, turn the crank.

And in the next cage, we have the hippopotamus who has a square asshole and eats mud. Every time he shits, he shits bricks. Hence the pyramids and Stanford University. Larry, turn the crank.

And in the next cage, we have the elephant who, strange enough, holds intercourse but one each hundred years; but when — he — do — He DO! — and how he does enjoy it. Larry, turn the crank.

And in the next cage we have the rhinoceros, the wealthiest animal alive. His name comes from *Rhino* meaning money, and *sore ass* meaning piles — hence, piles of money. See his ass in the bank.

ca 1928

This recitation is from the ca. 1928 "The Book of a Thousand Laughs."[111] In truth, it is a version of an entirely different monologue usually known as "Daniel in the Lion's Den." Nonetheless, the "piles of money" joke shows up as in the "Wild West Show."

The Stereopticon Lecture

Mr. Patrick O'Brien had recently purchased a worn-out stereopticon outfit and with the assistance of his friend Larry, he was giving his first public exhibition, it being at a church social. When O'Brien purchased the outfit he was given verbal instruction in regard to the lecture which accompanied the pictures, but the most of the lecture had already slipped his mind. After the usual preliminary arrangements had all been made, O'Brien stepped forward and made the following announcement:

"Ladies and gentlemen and little children; I take great pleasure in introducing to you our celebrated pictures which have been exhibited before all the crowned heads of Europe, Asia, Africa and parts of New Jersey. The pictures are principally taken from biblical history, and are interspersed with others taken from 'Goldsmith's Animated Nature.'

"The first picture which I shall show you represents 'Denial in the Lion's Den.' Denial not giving a damn for the Denial; you will easily distinguish Denial by the green coat he wears. Denial was a Kerry man. Whether the lions in the background bitin' the fleas have anything to do with the picture I don't know.

"In the morning Nebuchadhezzar came to Denial and said; 'Look out, Denial, the lions will bite you.' 'Bite me arse' said Denial, 'they have no teeth.' 'Who pulled them,' said the king. 'The Lard pulled them,' said Denial. And the king said 'Denial, hadst thou not displeased me you would not have been cast into this dark hole'. 'What hole?' said Denial. 'Arse hole' said the king, and the drinks was on Denial."

At this part of the lecture several in the audience commenced to show signs of uneasiness, and O'Brien stepped to the front of the platform and said: "Let no one leave their seats as the best part of the show is yet to come.

"Larry, turn the crank just a little more — that will do.

"The next picture, ladies and gentlemen, is Faith, Hope and Charity. Look at it, boys, look at it; ain't it grand? The one on the left with the pretty face is Faith, the one in the center with the big tits is Hope, but Lard Gard, boys, look at the arse on Charity. Arrah Gorrah, boys, if I was only there.

"Let no one leave their seats. The next picture is taken from Goldsmith's Animated Nature, and represents the Alligator, a denizen of the Nile; he has a wide and expansive smile and it is said that he do agitate the waters when he enters the satchel of his mate.

"Larry, turn the crank just a little more.

"The next picture represents the Gorilla of the African forests who, in certain seasons of the year, seizes the female of his species and flies to the top of the trees with her, and, amidst loud cries of "A-yum-yum," puts the blocks to her.

"Larry, turn the crank.

"Ah, this picture, ladies and gentlemen, represents the Kangaroo of Australia. It is said that he takes a leap of forty and seven feet like the devil going through Athlone, and every time he leaps he farts and every time he farts he leaps. Long lectures have been delivered and large books have been written as to whether he leaps to fart or farts to leap."

At this part a large number of the audience manifested a desire to leave the hall, which had the effect of making O'Brien mad, so he stepped to the front of the platform and in a very severe tone and injured manner spoke as follows.

"Ladies and gentlemen, during my long career before the public, this is the first time that I have ever noticed marks of disapprobation among the audience. Let no one leave their seats, the best part of the show is yet to come.

"Larry, turn the crank, not quite so far; ah, that will do.

"This picture represents the 'Mastodon' or Mammoth, of holy writ. It is similar to the elephant of our days, only it has no hair on it. It is said he has intercourse with the female of his species but once in a thousand years, but when he do, Lard Gard, how he do enjoy himself.

"Let no one leave their seats.

"The next picture represents the Rhinoceros, which means the richest animal in the world; the words 'Rhino' is from Latin and money. 'Oceros' a sore arse, means piles — Piles of Money."

"Larry, turn the crank."

1929

Attributed to Frank Shay, this variant is from "A Collection of Sea Songs and Ditties, From the Stores of Dave E. Jones."[112] It was dated by John Patrick to 1929. Song number 10 on page 9 of this mimeographed collection is a version of "Cats in the Rooftops," which has this line suggesting the growing influence of "The Wild West Show":

The rhino sore ass so it seems
Very seldom has wet dreams.
But when he does, he comes in streams
As he revels in the joys of fornication.

1929 [?]

This is the fullest text of this cante-fable (though lacking the cante) recovered.[113] In this version, Professor Simpson falls ill, and his assistant, Larry, agrees to deliver his own interpretation of Simpson's monologue with accompanying stereopticon slides. It too borrows from, or lends to the "Menagerie/Wild West Show" complex. Slide one is of the three graces: Faith, Hope and Charity.

> "Get on to the tits of Hope — stop your laughing there, you boys in the front row, these are not common whores — and what do you think of the ass on Grace; but I tell you confidentially, gentlemen, Charity is the best screwing. *Larry, turn the crank.*
>
> "The next picture is of a wild cat. Note that the difference between a wild cat and a tame one, is that the wild cat has no touch hole, therefore he can't shit, and that is what makes him wild. *Larry, turn the crank.*
>
> "Next picture, ladies and gentlemen, is the picture of Adam and Eve in the Garden of Eden. You see Adam and Eve with all the foliage and leaves around them and at first sight it seems as if they had nothing on at all; but if you look very closely, ladies, you will see that Adam has a hard-on. *Larry, turn the crank.*
>
> "Next picture, ladies and gentlemen, is the picture of the Ostrich. He is a native of the North Pole. He has a habit when being pursued, of sticking his beak in the sand and whistling the German National Hymn through his touch-hole; for what reason, goodness only knows. *Larry, turn the crank.*
>
> "Next picture, ladies and gentlemen, is a picture of a zebra, a native of the middle of Asia. He has stripes around his whole body from the tip of his nose to the end of his tail. The stripes are so tight that every time he winks, he jerks himself off. The little boys of the desert have a habit of throwing sand in his eyes, to see him in the act of masturbation. *Larry, turn the crank.*
>
> "Next picture, ladies and gentlemen, is a picture of two laughing hyenas. They are natives of Asia Minor. They have erections but twice a year and intercourse but once a year, but what the hell they see to laugh at in that, goodness only knows. *Larry, turn the crank.*
>
> "Next picture, ladies and gentlemen, is a picture of the hippopatamus [sic]. A powerful beast of the wilds of Turkey. His hide is so thick

that [it] cannot be pierced by spear or arrow. In the pursuit of this animal, the natives chase him across the desert, ticking his ass with a ten dollar ostrich feather; when up goes his tail, in goes the arrow, and the monarch of the desert lies prostrate.

"Next picture, ladies and gentlemen, is a picture of a crane. He is found in all parts of the world, particularly in Highland Park. He feeds on fishes, bugs, reptiles and all things that crawl on the ground. In the pursuit of his food one day, he found a very appetizing snake, caught him up, swallowed him and said, "Down you go." But the snake crawled through him and came out of his touch-hole. He grabbed him up again and says, "Down you go" and backs up against a fence, but the snake came through his touch-hole and then through a hole in the fence. Very mad, he grabbed him up again and says 'Down you go,' and sits himself in the sand. Again, the snake crawls out through his touch-hole into the sand. In a rage he finds him, swallows him and very quickly sticks his beak in his touch-hole, and as the snake comes out, swallows him again and says, "Now loop-the-loop, you son of a bitch." *Larry, turn the crank.*

"Next picture, ladies and gentlemen, is a picture of a rhinosoorass [sic]. He is a native of the middle of Africa. His skin is so thick that it cannot be pierced by bullets or swords. The name rhinosoorass [sic] is derived from two Greek words, rhino, meaning money; and soreass [sic] meaning piles; piles of money. That's what he cost. *Larry, turn the crank.*

1930?

Undated 78 rpm record that could only loosely be dated from 1930–1955. Swarthmore College had an annual show entitled "The Hamburg Show." The text of the song began, "We're off to see the Hamburg Show."

ca. 1933 ff.?

John Patrick has in his collection of erotica the "Forester's Songbook," a typescript or mimeographed copy that mentions the Civilian Conservation Corps at Iowa State University. It gives only the chorus:

The Hamburg Show

We're going to the Hamburg Show,
To see the elephant and the wild kangaroo

And we'll all stick together
In fair or stormy weather
For we're going to see the whole show through.

1936

A novel released this year — though harkening back to WWI — contains this example of "outside narration":

> Step up, gents. Step up. One and all. No trickery. No deception whatsoever.
>
> Step up and see Professor Jimmy Golden wrassle the distilled grape. Golden, the Hun tamer. Step up… "…See the *rhinoceros*. The name comes from the Greeks, *rhino* meaning jack… the second syllable meanin' heaps, mounds or piles, and *piles of money* is what he costs. See the zebra, the wild ass from the desert of Africa…"[114]

ca. World War II

Yet another fusion of "Larry, Turn the Crank" and "The Wild West Show" was collected by Martin Page from former active service members. Page entitled his variant "The Menagerie."[115] Page argues (p. 121), "There was the mock lantern-slide show, 'The Menagerie,' whose origins go back to the First World War but which was revived and remained popular throughout the second."

> "Good evening, ladies and gentlemen. You can see before you the fabulous Phoenix. This North African bird, when feeling the approach of his end, flies round a tall palm tree in circles of decreasing radius and increasing velocity, finally flying up its own arsehole with a loud report and a cloud of smoke. Ernie, turn the crank.
>
> "This is the Oozalum bird, normally quite dumb. But when excited, it sticks its long bill into the mud of the seashore and whistles "God Save the King" out its arse — hence the trade winds. Ernie, turn the crank.
>
> "Here we have the hippopotamus, whose hide is so tough that no bullet can pierce, no spear penetrate. How then is it overcome? Ah ha! The wily natives are up to the dodge: They apply ginger to its touch-

hole. Up goes the tail — and in go the arrows. Not one, mind you, but in thousands; and the whole show is over. Ernie, turn the crank.

"The rhinoceros, ladies and gentlemen, is the richest animal in the world. Rhino equals money. Sore arse equals piles. Piles of money. Ernie, turn the crank.

"This large ape, the orang utang, inhabits the impenetrable forests of Borneo, but when overcome by his lust, descends to the plains in search of village maidens. He finds, feels, fondles and finally fucks them, exclaiming the while, in his own language, 'Yahoo, yahoo,' — which being interpreted, means 'By God, that's good.' Ernie, turn the crank.

"I would call your attention to the tight-skinned parrot. His skin is so tight that when he closes his eyes, he skins his prick, a drawback he bears with equanimity amounting to delight. His eyes are now closed, hence the odd smell. Madam, please stop your small boy throwing sand at him to make him blink. Ernie, turn the crank.

"Finally, the camel, who comes from the mighty Sahara Desert, where normal food is scarce. He eats sand, and has a triangular arse and shits bricks. Hence the Pyramids. Thank you, Ernie."

1944

This unattributed fragment was among the Richard Reuss papers.

Van Amberg is the man who goes to all the shows,
He walks into the lion's cage and tells you all he knows.
He puts his head in the lion's mouth and keeps it there a while
And when he takes it out again, he greets you with a smile.

CHORUS:
Oh, we'll all go to see Van Amberg's show,
See the lion and the wild kangaroo.
Yes, we'll all get together and we'll go
To see Van Amberg's show.

The lion in the next cage, most wonderful to relate,
Got awfully mad the other day and ate up its female mate.
Now don't you go near his cage, I warn you little boys,
For when he's mad he wags his tail and makes an awful noise.

"At Swarthmore College there is an annual event known as the Hamburg Show, which is a student-produced and student-written musical comedy. In conjunction with it we sing the following song, which I considered indigenous only to Swarthmore:

"Oh, we're going to the Hamburg Show,
See the lion and wild kangaroo.
And we'll all stick together in every kind of weather,
'Cause we're going to see the whole thing through.

"Imagine my surprise at hearing my father-in-law burst forth with the Van Amberg variation, which he had learned from his uncle."[116]

1952

This version, entitled "The Hamburg Show," was printed in a small, uncredited collection entitled "Old American Ballads." Distinguished by its unusual chorus, it dates from 1952 and the Korean War.

> CHORUS:
> Hey, Hey, Where we going?
> We're goin' to the Hamburg Show
> To see the lion, the wild kangaroo.
> Through fair and stormy weather,
> We'll all stick together
> 'Cause we're gonna see the whole show through.
> Well, well, the gang's all here.
> What the hell do we care:
> Damn it to hell, we don't care now.
> Hail, Hail, the gang's all here,
> What the hell do we care now.
>
> Hey, hey, have you seen the spotted hyena;
> He has 365 spots, one for every day of the year.

What's that, lady? What does he do on Leap Year?
Lift up his tail, lift up his tail.
Hey, hey, where we goin'.

    Etc.

1955

"I spent the weekend of Nov. 10th in the Kappa Alpha Theta house at Northwestern.... Everyone started talking and laughing and someone started singing. This led to the singing of 'The Hamburg Show.' After they had stopped, they started telling me of the story of the famous song. It seems that a graduate of NU [Northwestern University], a man of about fifty-years old, wrote 99 verses to this song and all of them just as funny as the verses I have related."[117]

> CHORUS:
> We're off to the hamburg show [sic, lower case],
> To elephants and wild kangaroos.
> We'll all stick together in fair and stormy weather,
> And we'll all see the whole show through.
>
> VERSE:
> And now, ladies and gentlemen, we come to cage number one where we have the African kangaroo. When he jumps, he farts, and when he farts, he jumps. Now the question is does his jumping make him fart, or does his farting make him jump.
>
> And now, ladies and gentlemen, we come to cage number two where we have the Rhinosoreass. Rhino meaning hard-skin, sore ass meaning piles.
>
> And now, ladies and gentlemen, we come to cage number three where we have the crocodile. When he shits, he shits bricks. Hence the pyramids.

1955

> CHORUS:
> We're off to the Hamburg Show,
> See the elephant and the wild kangaroo,

And we'll all stick together in fair or stormy weather,
And we're going to see the whole show through.

> "Now step right up to the first tent, ladies and gentlemen, and see the male alligator. A wondrous creature is the male alligator and a boon to man. And do you know why? Well, I'll tell you. The female alligator lays one million eggs and the male alligator eats 999,999,999 of those eggs. And if the male alligator didn't, we'd be up to our ears in alligators.

> "Now step right up to the second tent, ladies and gentlemen, and see the Ki-Ki bird. Now the Ki-Ki bird lives only at the North Pole. This bird is very rare because he flies along over the icy land backwards and as he flies, he gives his famous call, "Ki-ki-ki-ki-Ki-rist but it's cold up here.[118]

Late 1950s

> "From my mother (!!) I suppose in the late 1950s in Nottingham [UK]:

> "Either the onga-wonga bird or the foo-foo bird (she was never quite sure) '…which flies around in ever-diminishing circles, finally disappearing up its own posterior orifice, from which advantageous position it hurls shit and derision at its baffled pursuers."[119]

Late 1950s

"I heard and joined in the chorus in the late 1950s what seems from other contributions to be a pretty standard version of "Wild West Show." It was sung in the bars of the male Glasgow University Student's Union, but I first heard it about 1958 from Hamish Imlach."[120]

> CHORUS:
> We're off to see the Wild West Show,
> The elephant and the kangaroo-oo-oo-oo.
> Never mind the weather, so long as we're together.
> We're off to see the Wild West Show.

> Patter 'verses' each began with:
> "And in the next cage, ladies and gentlemen, we have the _____."

The audience responded with 'The ____?"
"Yes, ladies and gentlemen, the ____."

"These included 'the Winky-Wanky Bird, the Fukawee tribe, the orang-utang, and another, I think, the Gee-raffe with the punch line "the high balls are on me."

ca. 1960

"Most of the verses I knew from ca. 1960 have been mentioned: Giraffe, Rhino-sore-arse, Fukawi tribe, winky-wanky bird, ooh-aah bird, are the ones I remember."[121]

ca. 1960

In an email, Steve Gardham sketched the formula of stanzas with which he was familiar as a youthful rugby player in the UK:

The Wild West Show

CHORUS:
Oh, we're off to see the wild west show,
The elephant and the kangaroo-oo-oo,
Never mind the weather as long as we're together,
We're off to see the wild west show.

> Solo: And in the first cage, ladies and gentlemen, we have the fantastic oomiegoolie bird.

> Audience, in chorus: Fantastic, impossible, what the fucking hell's that?

> Solo: Yes, the fantastic Oomiegoolie bird, so-called because it has little wings and short legs, and as it flies over the treetops [coming in for a landing?], you can hear it cry, "Ooh, me goolies, ooh me goolies!"

Additional verses considered the attributes of the winky wanky bird, the fuckawee tribe, the constipated elephant, the orangutang, and the Australian spiral bird.

1962

CHORUS:
We're off to the [Hamburg?] zoo
To see the elephants and the wild Kangaroo.
And we'll all sing together
Through fair and stormy weather,
'Cause we're off to the Hamburg Zoo.

And on your right, ladies and gentlemen, we have the world's only hippopotamus to be impregnated by a monkey. You might say someone put him up to it.

In this corner, ladies and gentlemen, we have the Ooo-ee bird, who feeds only on elephant ears. He masticates them in his oral cavity. They peek behind his tonsils, and slither down the esophagus. They say hello to the stomach and pass on through the pyloric sphincter. They go round and round in the small intestine; play peek-a-boo in the large intestine. And, well, you know the rest. It just waits to fly over (a member of the audience's) head.[122]

1962

The Wild West Show[123]

CHORUS:
Oh! we're off to see the Wild West Show
The elephants and the kangaroo.
No matter what the weather,
As long as we're together,
We're off to see the Wild West Show.

Ladies and gentlemen, may I introduce to you the orangatang, the only animal in captivity with glass balls. Now when this amazing creature swings through the forest his balls go o-rang-a-tang.

Ladies and gentlemen, may I introduce to you the Bengal tiger. This animal is the only 300-pound pussy that will eat you.

Ladies and gentlemen, may I introduce to you the foom-foom-bird. [The foom-foom-bird] flies in flocks of three, and when confronted with an adversary, the third foom-foom-bird and the second foom-foom-bird fly up each other's asshole. And the first foom-foom-bird flies up the third foom-foom-bird's asshole, leaving their adversary in total darkness.

Ladies and gentlemen, may I introduce to you the baboon, the only animal in captivity with rubber balls. Now when this amazing creature swings through the forest, his balls go baboon, baboon, baboon.

Ladies and gentlemen, may I introduce you to the le-o-pard, the only animal in captivity with one spot on him for every day of the year. (One person in the audience asks about February 29th. The speaker replies: Assistant, lift his tail for February 29th.

1963

The cante-fable, that is, stories with songs and/or choruses interspersed in the text, are relatively few in Anglo-American folk song. Edith Fowke collected two in Ontario, from informants who might have lived in a French-speaking community and there might have acquired the sung-spoken story-form.

The Wild West Show[124]

CHORUS:
We're off to see the Wild West Show,
The elephant and the kangaroo-oo-oo-oo,
Never mind the weather, as long as we're together,
We're off to see the Wild West Show.

"And in this cage, ladies and gentlemen, may I present a game of euchre. It seems that an elephant met a mouse on the jungle path one day, and the mouse said to the elephant, "Can you play euchre?" To which the elephant answered, "No, I cannot." So the mouse said, "Then I'll teach you." So he [the mouse] crawled in his trunk and out his ass, and said "That's one trick for me." The elephant said, "I think I'm learning. Will you do it again?" So the mouse climbed into the elephant's trunk and out his ass and said, "That's two tricks for me." At which the elephant said, "I think I catch on. Let's play." So the mouse climbed into the elephant's trunk and the elephant stuck his trunk up his ass and said, "You're euchred."

"Now, in this cage, ladies and gentlemen, may I present the rhinosauras. Now, as you know, in ancient times it was thought that the rhinosauras, which has a horn upon its nose, could have the horn melted down and used for medicinal purposes. The ancient Chinese used to do this very thing and sold the product for great amounts of money. Therefore, it was they who gave it its title, taking the name from two derivatives: rhino, which is Greek for money, and sauras, while is Anglo-Saxon for piles. Rhinosauras — piles of money.

"And in this cage, ladies and gentlemen, may I present the mylar bird, Now the mylar bird is a bird which lives in the sandy desert areas of Australia, and in a clear day it will thrust its head into the sand and fart, and you can hear it for a mile or more.

"And in this cage, ladies and gentlemen, may I present the saga of how Tarzan got his yell. It seems that Tarzan and Jane were sitting beside a simple stream one day; Jane was swimming and Tarzan climbed out on the bank to eat a banana. Suddenly an agonized scream from the stream turned Tarzan around and there was Jane frantically swimming for shore, pursued by a great alligator, Tarzan grabbed a vine and swung out over the stream, screaming, "Jane, as I pass over, you grab the vine. OOOOOH! The vine, Jane, the vine!"

The Goldstein-Fowke notes comment that his is one of the few bawdy songs that is mainly excretory rather than sexual in nature. "It's a parody of a barker's spoken monologue that dwells on the peculiar habits — mostly scatological — of diverse birds and animals, interspersed with a sung chorus. The pattern is widespread, sometimes as 'The London Zoo,' 'The Hamburg Show,' or 'Larry, Turn the Crank.' Legman relates it to 'Humours of Bartholomew Fair' dating back at least to 1888."

1963 or 1964

Simon Furey contributed additional verses learned from "a fellow apprentice in Derby [UK]…"

"The winky-wanky bird: 'whose eyelids are connected to its organ;
when it winks it wanks, and when it wanks it winks'

"The oomigoolies bird: 'which sadly was born without legs,
And whenever it comes in to land, it cries "Oomigoolies! Oomigoolies!"'

"The constipated elephant: 'that has not shat in forty years.
Don't stand too near the back end, Madam! Too late! Dig her out!'"[125]

1964

In a letter from Gershon Legman to Richard Reuss written 21st July 1975, Legman noted ["The Wild West Show"] is another development from "The Hamburg Show." Legman — who dated this Australian text to 1964 — deemed "the responses of the audience (doubtless rugby teams, as you note) are a big element in my Australian texts and one of the funniest parts, e.g.

"Rec[itor]. Here, lydies and gentlemen, we have the Fuckawi Tribe.
"Aud[ience]. Fuckawi Tribe? Faaan-TAS-tick!! (screaming the "TAS")
"Rec. The three-foot Fuckawi tribe lives in deepest Africa where the grass is four feet high. — Comes up over their eyes! They run wildly through the tall grass, agitating their spears and shields, while shouting, We're the Fuckawi? We're the Fuckawi?"

Legman continued, "As the dialectical pronunciation of "we're" for "where" shows, this is as Austrylian [sic] as they make 'em! ... The audience also gives the "Wild West Show" chorus (sung) between animals, with variant end-line, "As long as we're together, bugger the bloody weather, We're off to see the Wild West Show!" (In fact, various dialects of English including the UK Midlands also pronounce "we're" rather than "where." Consequentially, the origins of "The Wild West Show" must remain obscure.)

1965

This text was sent by Professor Robert McFadden to folklorist and editor Judy McCulloh, who had transcribed the tune as sung at a Louisiana State University rugby gathering. Ms. McCulloh was impressed enough by the song to ask McFadden about it. McFadden wrote that he had learned the song in his native Belfast, Northern Ireland. That former rugby player and referee is now a professor emeritus at the University of Louisville. He sent these verses, used with his permission.

The Wild West Show

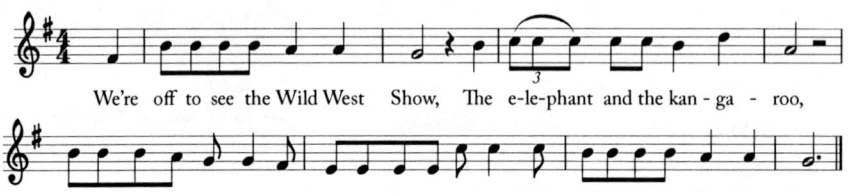

We're off to see the Wild West Show, The e-le-phant and the kan - ga - roo,
Ne-ver mind the wea-ther, as long as we're to- ge-ther, We're off to see the Wild West Show.

CHORUS:
We're off to see the Wild West Show, the elephant and the kangaroo,
Never mind the weather as long as we're together,
We're off to see the Wild West Show.

Narrator: In this cage, ladies and gentlemen, we have the _____.
Group: The _____? (Use ad libitum)
Narrator: Yes, the _____.
Group: Fantastic.

Narrator: The leopard. This animal lives in the deepest, darkest jungles of Africa and is a swift and vicious hunter. To fit it for this life, it is camouflaged, having spots all over his belly, 365 of them, one for every day of the year.
Member of Audience: "What about leap year?"
Narrator: "Lift up its tail."

Narrator: The Giraffe. (Description, elaborate or not, of the giraffe and/or its habitat) It is the only animal in the world who can walk into a bar and say, "The high balls are in me."

Polar Bear
To catch this animal, dig a hole in the ice and surround the whole with peas. When the bear comes up to take a pea, kick it in the ice hole.

The Lion
The lion is unique in the animal kingdom, being the only pussy in the world that will eat you.

The Orang Outang
This animal has balls of brass, and as it swings from branch in the jungle, you can hear his balls clashing together, orang outang, orang outang.

Crocogater
This is the meanest animal in the world. It has the head of an alligator at one end and the head of a crocodile at the other. "How does it shit?"[sic] "It doesn't. That's why it's so mean."

Old Man from Borneo
This [wild]man has an enormous penis, 18 inches long and 4 1/2 inches in diameter. "What about his balls?"
"He has none; that's what makes him wild."

Fat Assed Lady
The fattest woman in the world. She has a large W tattooed on one buttock, the same on the other, and when she bends over. WOW.

The Fat Lady's Sister
She has "Merry Christmas" tattooed on one buttock and "Happy New Year" on the other, and she says, "Won't you come up and see me between the holidays."

Fukawee Tribe
This tribe of pygmies lives in tall grass country and they often get lost. Then they jump up and down, shouting their tribal cry: "Fuckawee, where the fuckawee?"

The Ooh Ah Bird
The female lives in the north pole, the male at the south pole; once a year they meet at the equator. Then can be heard their plaintive cry: Ooh Ah. Ooh ah.

Omagoomla Bird
This bird has very large testicles and very short legs, and every time it lands, it cries, "Omagoomla, Omagoomla."

College Man
This animal will mate only with a female who has a sense of humor, so as soon as he meets a likely partner, he gives her a testicle."

Itchy Kitchy Koo Bird
[This bird] flies in ever decreasing circles until it sticks its head up its own ass, then shouts, "Itchy kitchy Koo." This means little to us, but to other itchy kitchy koo birds, it means "I can't see for shit."

The Mathematical Impossibility
[This] is a little girl who was ate [eight] before she was seven.

The French Limousine
[The French limousine is] very large. One can get eight [ate] in the front and 69 in the back.

The Winky Wanky Bird
[This bird] has its foreskin attached to its eyelid. Every time it winks, it wanks, and every time it wanks, it winks. Don't throw sand in the bird's eyes.

1965

This version of "The Wild West Show," learned at the University of Maryland, ca. 1965, came with a headnote: "This song is one of the most popular and is seldom left out. There are hundreds of verses. The chorus is sung by all, as are the prearranged reactions (incredible, fantastic, etc). The verses are spoken by an individual in his own words after he has raised his hand and waited his turn. This goes on until everyone is tired of the song. I have known it to continue for forty-five minutes or more."

> Chorus (Repeated after each verse):
> Oh, we're off to see the wild west show,
> The elephant and the kangaroo.
> Never mind the weather
> As long as we're together.
> We're off to see the wild west show.

Leader: And in this corner, ladies and gentlemen, we have again the historic event, the battle between the ostrich and the snake.

Group: Fantastic, incredible, no shit, what the bloody fuck is that? (This response will be repeated through the entire song/performance.)

Leader: Round one. Anyway, the ostrich comes out of his corner. The ostrich glared at the snake, the snake glares at the ostrich. The ostrich leaps at the snake. The snake jumps to the side but the ostrich grabs him anyway and gobbles him up. However, the snake, being a very wily snake, goes down the esophagus, round and round the intestine, and out the fundamental orifice. Round one for the snake.

Group: (Cheering, applause)

Leader: Round two. The ostrich comes out of his corner, the snake comes of his corner. The ostrich glares at the snake. The snake glares at the ostrich. But the ostrich this time immediately leaps at the snake, gobbles up the snake again, and puts his fundamental orifice against a wooden paneling. But the snake, being a very wily snake, goes down the esophagus, round and round the intestine, and out a knothole in the paneling. [Round two to the snake.]

Group: Cheering, applause.

Leader: Round three. The ostrich comes out of his corner, the snake comes out of his corner. The snake glares at the ostrich; the ostrich leaps at the snake. The ostrich again gobbles up the snake and this time puts his own head up his fundamental orifice, and says, "Now loop-the-loop, you bugger."

Chorus

Leader: And in this corner we have the giraffe.

Group: Fantastic, incredible, no shit, what the bloody fuck is that?

Leader: The giraffe is a very wily animal, the only one who can walk into a bar and say, "The high balls are on me."

Chorus

Leader: Roll up, roll up, ladies and gentlemen. In this cage we have the mountain goat.

Group: The mountain goat?

Leader: Yes, the mountain goat.

Group: Fantastic, etc.

Leader: The mountain goat is a very agile animal, lives in the upper Alps, the upper Andes, the upper Himalayas. As I said, ladies and gentlemen, this animal jumps from precipice to precipice and back to piss again.

Leader: And in this corner. We have the ke-ke bird.
Group: The ke-ke bird?
Leader: Yes, the ke-ke bird.
Group: Fantastic, etc.
Leader: The ke-ke bird is a very unusual bird. All it does is fly around the north pole and slide down icebergs. And then it goes to the top of the iceberg and slides down again. And then you can hear its cry going across the frozen north, going "ke-ke-kerist, it's cold."

1965

Richard Reuss's handwritten notation at top of first page reads, "John Walsh, Urbana, Ill., 12-4-65."

The Wild West Show[126]

Oh, we're off to see the wild west show,
The elephant and the kangaroo-o[o]-o[o].
Never mind the weather, as long as we're together,
We're off to see the wild west show.

1) The Barker: In this cage, ladies and gentlemen, we have the African Giraffe. (A marginal note states: "pronounced gee'-raff — all animal names are exaggerated in the manner of a sideshow barker.")

All: The African Giraffe? [Echoing the pronunciation]
Barker: Yes, ladies and gentlemen, the African Giraffe.
All: Fantastic.
Barker: Now the African Giraffe is a very generous fellow. He's the only animal who walks into a bar and says, "Okay, guys. The highballs are on me."
Chorus

2) Barker: And here, ladies and gentlemen, is the African leopard (pronounced: Lee-o-pard)
All: The African leopard?
Barker: Yes, ladies and gentlemen, the African leopard.
All: Fantastic.
Barker: Ladies and gentlemen, we have the most amazing animal in the word. He has 365 spots, one for every day in the year. (From the crowd

comes a high voice: "But sir, what about Leap Year?" Lift his tail, lady, lift his tail.

CHORUS

In the same spirit, the amazed tourists are led past such animals as:

3) The Concentric Bird — this bird, when attacked, flies in ever-decreasing circles until at last it flies up its own anal orifice, thereby leaving its enemies in the dark.

4) The Orangutang — whose balls are made of brass and dangle three feet below his ass. And when he swings through the jungle, they clang together with the noise "Orang-Utang, Orang-Utang."

5) The Barumba-Barumba bird — evidentially a related species, since it also has brass balls dangling three feet below his ass. When he flies low over the tin village roofs, his balls go "Barumba-Barumba."

6) The Kiwi Bird — This little fellow isn't much to look at — only two feet tall — but he has the longest pecker in the world.

7) Santa Claus — who only comes once a year, and then it's down a chimney.

8) The Tattooed Lady — one her left buttock is tattooed a "W" and on her right buttock is tattooed another "W" and when she bends over: WOW!

9) The Tattooed Lady's Assistant — on one leg is tattooed "Merry Christmas." On the other leg is tattooed "Happy New Year" and she cordially invites you to drop in between the seasons [sic, for holidays].

10) The Fuckawe Pygmies — who live in the plains of Central Africa, where the grass grows three feet high. The pygmies are only two-feet high, and go around saying, "Where the Fuckawee."

11) The Homosexual Spider — who is called by that name because it has a funny habit of playing with other spiders' flies.

12) The Homosexual Indian — a brave fucker. (In a nearby cage is the 97-pound weakling who went to Alaska. He came back a husky fucker.) [Cray — the 97-pound weakling is a reference to a long-running ad placed in comic books by a body-building program.]

13) The Homosexual Mailman — another denizen of this queer corner of the zoo, who is always putting his hand in mail boxes. [An aural pun]

14) The Piebald Pony — so called, because his balls are 3.1416 inches in diameter.

15) The Armadillo — These little creatures travel head-to-tail in a long line. When danger threatens, the last one runs into the asshole of the next in line, who, in turn, runs up the asshole of the one in front of him and so on up to the very first one, who cries out, "Armadillo!" This may not mean much to you, but in Armadillo language it means, "Jesus Christ, I'm buggered."

16) The fight between the Ostrich and the Python — These animals are deadly enemies. Ding! Round one. They come out and eye each other warily. Suddenly the python leaps into the open mouth of the ostrich, slithers down his esophagus, round his intestines, and out his fundamental orifice. Round one to the python. Ding! Round two. They eye each other warily, and again the python leaps in[to] the mouth of the ostrich, goes down his esophagus, round his intestines and out his fundamental orifice. Round two to the python. Ding! Round three. They come out, looking very determined. Once again the python jumps down the open throat if the ostrich, goes down his esophagus and around his intestines. Suddenly the ostrich puts his head around his own anal orifice, looks the python in the eye, and says, "Loop-the-loop, you bugger."

17) The Ooh-Aah Bird — who lays big, square eggs, and then [says] "Ooh-Aah."

18) The Lion — the only pussy that eats you.

19) The African Ostrich — who lays round eggs three feet in diameter; you ought to see his oss-stretch.

20) The African kee-kee bird — he lives on the tipmost top of the tipmost top of Kilimanjaro and when he slides down on his ass on the glaciers, ice and frozen lakes, he hollers, "Kee-kee-kee-kee-rist it's cold up here!"

21) The Winky-Wanky bird — who has his foreskin tied to his eyebrow, so when he winks he wanks, and when he wanks he winks.

22) Tarzan and His Ape Call — Tarzan got his ape-call in the following manner: One day, he decided to teach his mate, Jane, how to swing through the jungle as he did. "First, Jane, you grab the vine — the vine, Jane, the vine — No, Jane, the vi—Ooooo-eeeeyah!"

23) The Polar Bear — The Eskimos catch these animals by first chopping a hole in the ice, and then sprinkling a can of peas around the edge. When the bear comes down [up?] to take a pea, they kick him in the ice hole. This is similar to the method used in Africa to trap elephants, wherein the natives dig a big hole in which they burn large logs until the bottom is coated with a thick layer of ash. Then a can of peas is sprinkled [around the hole] and when the elephant comes to take a pea, they kick him in the ash hole.

24) The African Elephant — This animal only defecates once a year, and — Stand back, boy! As I was saying, when he does — Stand back, boy! Oops, too late. Dig him out.[126]

1966

"The critic Kenneth Burke knew at least one line of the piece. '[L]ogic is made comically, Aristophanically supreme in the vulgar lines about "the fabulous bird that eats sand and s—— [shots] bricks, and *hence* the pyramids."[126]

1968–1970

"Lots of people contributed verses. The way us New York area folks did this was as follows:

Leader: In this cage we have the incredible Fugawi bird.
Crowd: The Fugawi bird?
Leader: Yes, the Fugawi bird.

Crowd: Fantastic…
And the leader tells the rest, up to the punch line.
Everyone groans, and then we all sing the chorus:

"We're off to see the Wild West show,
The elephants and the kangaroos.
Never mind the weather, as long as we're together
 We're off to see the Wild West show."

And the next person chimes in with:
"And in this cage…"

"There must be hundreds of verses."[128]

1967

In the fall of 1967, Stephen Anaya took a folklore class from Richard Reuss at UCLA. Anaya's notes state he collected no fewer than twenty-seven different verses of "The Wild West Show" from ten informants whom he described as upper-middle-class rugby players, most of whom would go on to become professional, white-collar workers. All but one of Anaya's informants was a member of the then-San Fernando Valley State (now California State University, Northridge) rugby club. One was a member of the UCLA rugby club.

Anaya's field notes continued: "It seems the more debased the song becomes, the more enjoyable and spontaneous the singing becomes. This is the time of verse-inventions, and also a time of verse-shock. For example, some verses have a shock value especially in mixed company. The ruggers know this and delight in making shocking remarks and gestures with the singing."[129]

According to Anaya, "Most of the verses have been learned at inter-team rugby parties and beer busts after rugby matches."

Anaya added that "many verses drop from view in individual clubs. There is a tendency for my informants to remember the simpler, and the oldest forms of verses. For example, in this collection, these are the most numerous: 'The Orang-A-Tang,' 'Yumac Bird,' 'Lion,' 'No-No Bird,' 'Camuel,' and the 'Ubangi Tribe.'… The newer verses, I found, tend to be more complex and longer in content. Because of this, their life history within the song may not last."[130]

Wild West Show

CHORUS: (Sung by the group)
We're off to see the Wild West Show,
The elephants and the kangor-oo-oos,
No matter what the weather,
As long as we're together,
We're off to see the Wild West Show.

Barker: Step right up, ladies and gentlemen, boys and girls. In this corner we have a gee-raft.
Group: (Loudly) A Gee-raft!! Fantastic!! What the hell is a gee-raft?
Barker: A gee-raft is a strange and interesting creature found on the central plains of Africa — But that's not what's so unusual 'bout this animal. This is the only animal in the animal kingdom that can go into a bar and say, "The highballs are on me!!"
Group: Ahhhhhh. Fuck. (Group picks up quickly the chorus)

Subsequent verses follow the same pattern of call-and-response.

> The Ooh-Ahh bird is an interesting animal in the fact that the female of the species weighs only five pounds, and the egg she lays weighs ten pounds. As she lays the huge egg she can be heard screaming, "Ooooo" then "Ahhhhhh."

> The midget is not like any of the other little people. You see the midget weighs a grand total of 30 pounds. His testicles weigh 15 pounds of the total. As you can see by now, the midget is half-nuts.

> The rat-tat-tat bird is quite rare. You see the bird flying at night just over corrugated rooftops. He does it for a reason of self-stimulation. The bird's height is two feet but the length of his sexual appendage, his cock, that is, is six feet. He zooms in low — about three inches — over the corrugated rooftops at 75 miles per hour and if you are in the house you can hear it buzz by: Rat-tat-tat, rat-tat-tat.

> The camuel is a very practical animal found in North Africa. You see, the camuel is the only animal that can dry hump with another camuel across an entire desert.

The laughing hyena (pronounced: hy-een-u-a) is a cousin of the wild dog. He lives in Africa and hasn't fornicated, defecated or masturbated for five years, and what's he laughing at, I'll never know.

The no-no bird is found only Guinea. The bird is peculiar because it has a three-inch body length with a 10-inch phallic length, and every time he has to land, he goes "No, no, no!"

The yes-yes bird is the female counterpart of the no-no bird. She hides and jumps out just before he lands, [and] spreads her legs to assure fertilization and the procreation of the species.

The lion is found in the deserts of South African desert country. The lion is strange and belongs in our show because it is the only 250-pound pussy that eats you.

The homosexual spider is a very peculiar insect. He is the only spider that specializes in eating [sic] other spiders' flies.

The Yumac bird is an interesting animal. This bird is native to the Japanese Islands. He is very anti-Chinese because he flies over crowded Oriental cities, dropping shit on people, screaming at the top of his lungs, "Fuck Yumac."

Ostrich-snake combat, though in this case the ostrich cries, "Circulate, you bloody bastard!" and for ingenuity the ostrich is awarded the match.

1967

Anaya's informant, who learned this in Dundee, Scotland, in 1963, knew the verse about the Tattooed Lady (between holidays), Orang-A-tang and Lion (250 pound pussy). Then the informant contributed these unusual verses:

The fu-fu bird is a strange animal that flies to great altitudes, sometimes 20,000 to 25,000 feet. He then dives at the speed of 750 miles per hour and just misses hitting the ground. As he pulls out of the dive, he can be heard saying, "Fu, fu, fuck that was close." (See 1952 text from the Korean war.)

The Sandwich Bird is found in Australia. It is extremely rare. It is the most sexually frustrated animal on earth. All day it flies over the bleak desert screaming, "Eat me! Eat me!" (Said with a high-pitched voice.)

The Yumac Bird is a strange animal that flies over the forest. When he sees an enemy, he flips the bird, and cries out, "Fuck Yumac! Fuck Yumac!"

The Yumac Bird is found in Central America. Known because it sleeps primarily during the day. If awakened in the daylight hours, the bird becomes very annoyed, and flies through the jungle screaming, "Fuck Yumac! Fuck Yumac!"

The next three were learned in a pub near Liverpool by RF and set down by Stephen Anaya.

The Russian robin is a strange and interesting bird. He is the national bird of the Communist revolution. One day the White Russians captured a young Bolshevik soldier. The soldier was condemned to die. But before his death, he was hung up on a scaffold and publicly castrated. Unbeknownst to the populace in the square, the Russian robin had landed on the scaffolding. The bird had never been known to make a sound or a cry, but the proceedings had shocked the bird so much that he began to cry out that great anti-czarist slogan: "Kut-ya-kok-av, kut-ya-kok-av." This united the peasants, and helped get rid of the czarist factions.

The woman sheriff is a very strange person to have in a western town. She is unique, you might say. Not unique in the fact she's a woman, but unique in the fact that all the men in town are dying to get in her posse.

The Russian yellow-bellied breast sucker is a bird peculiar to only the Soviet Union. In the summer it flies up from its nesting grounds on the Caspian Sea, north, to Moscow. It hovers over Red Square till it spies a flat-chested Russian woman walking in the square. The yellow-bellied breast sucker loses altitude and alights on the certain woman's shoulder, screaming, "Hoo bit'ya titsov! Hoo bit'ya titsov!"

The Orang-A-Thud is just like the Orang-A-Tang except that the Orang-A-Thud has one huge brass ball and one punching bag. And as he swings through the trees his balls go arang-a-thud, arang-a-thud!

1968

As printed in "Fester 1968," a publication by the mock "Society for the Promotion of Immoral Impulses and the Stamp Out Virginity Society, at their unregistered office somewhere in New Zealand."[131] This is a summary of otherwise unreported verses:

The Wild West Show

Speaker: Here, ladies and gentlemen, we have the hippopotamus.
Group: The hippopotamus?
Speaker: Yes, the hippopotamus is an amazing animal. When his eyes are open, its arsehole is closed. And when its eyes are closed its arsehole is open. Someone threw pepper in its eyes, and, Christ, he's got diarrhoea!

Chorus:
Oh, we're off to see the wild west show, [sic]
The elephant and the kangaroo-oo-oo.
Never mind the weather,
We're all in this together,
We're off to see the wild west show.

Barker: Here, ladies and gentlemen, we have the sphinx.
Audience: The sphinx?
Barker: Yes, then sphinx is an amazing animal. Yes, it is the only animal with a triangular arsehole. It shits bricks, hence pyramids!

Barker: Here, ladies and gentlemen, we have the elephant.
Audience: The elephant?
Barker: Yes, the elephant is an amazing animal. It eats twelve hours a day, but only shits once a week. And when it shits… Move away there, sonny. As I was saying, it eats all week and only shits… Please move away, sonny. And when it shits, it shits… Has anyone got a shovel?

Barker: Here, ladies and gentlemen, we have the shark.
Audience: The shark?
Barker: Yes, the shark is an amazing fish. It follows ships and it eats and secretes semen.

Barker: Here, ladies and gentlemen, we have the proud elephant.
Audience: The proud elephant?
Barker: Yes, the proud elephant is an amazing animal. He lies upside down in the jungle with his balls in the air. And then we have the biggest balls-up in the jungle.[132]

Barker: Here, ladies and gentlemen, we have the tiger.
Audience: The tiger?
Barker: Yes, the tiger is an amazing animal. He is the only animal with stripes on his cock to measure penetration.

Barker: Here, ladies and gentlemen, we have the sardine.
Audience: The sardine?
Barker: Yes, the sardine is an amazing fish. He leads a sordid life. He is found in the most peculiar circumstances, lying head to tail in sticky stuff.

Barker: Here, ladies and gentlemen, we have the ostrich.
Audience: The ostrich?
Barker: Yes, the ostrich is a most remarkable bird. It gets his head under the sand and its arse up,
Waiting, and waiting, and waiting ...

Here, ladies and gentlemen, we have the cryptic church mouse.
The cryptic church mouse?
Yes, the cryptic church mouse is a remarkable animal. He crept into the crypt, crapped, and crept out.

1968

The Wild West Show[133]

CHORUS:
Oh, we're off to see the Wild West Show
The elephant and the kangaroo

Never mind the weather
As long as we're together
We're off to see the Wild West Show.

"Now here, ladies and gentlemen, in the first cage we have the laughing hyena. This animal lives in the mountains and once every year comes down to eat. Once every two years he comes down to drink and once every three years he comes down for sexual intercourse. What the ****** [goddam] hell he has to laugh about, I don't know.

And in the next cage we have the giraffe. This creature is the most popular animal in the animal kingdom. Why? Every time he goes into a bar he says, "The highballs are on me."

And here, ladies and gentlemen, we have the urangutang. As this animal proceeds from branch [sic, to branch], swinging through the forest, his balls [go] urang-u-tang, urang-u-tang.

And in the next cage we have the Oster-reich. This animal, at the first sign of danger, buries its head in the sand and whistles through the *whole* [hole] of the afternoon.

And in the next cage we have the Rhino Sauras. This animal is reputed to be the richest in the world. Its name is derived from the Latin — rhino meaning money and sore**** [arse] meaning piles, hence piles of money.

And here we have the Keerie Bird. This bird lives in the Antarctic. And every time it comes in to land on the ice, it says, "Keerie, keerie, keer-ist it's cold."

And in the next cage we have the leopard. Yes, the leopard on its coat has one spot for every day of the year. What about a Leap Year? George, lift up the leopard's tail.

And in this cage we have the Winky Wanky Bird. By some strange happening, the nervous system of this bird's eyelids is connected to its foreskin. Every time it winks, it wanks and every time it wanks, it winks. You, boy, stop throwing sand in the bird's eyes.

And here is the elephant. The elephant has a ginormous appetite. In one day it eats two tons of hay, one dozen bunches of bananas and twenty buckets of rice. Madam, don't stand too near the elephant's backside. Madam — madam. Too late, George, dig her out.

And here, ladies and gentlemen, we have Oozle Woozle Bird. These birds fly in a line ahead formation and, at the first sign of danger, the last bird flies up the **** [arse] of the bird in front and so on up the line. The remaining bird then flies round in ever decreasing circles, finally disappearing up its own orifice from which position it proceeds to shower **** [shit] and derision in all directions.

And in the next cage we have the Triangular. This animal has a triangular orifice — hence the Pyramids and the sign of the Y.W.C.A.[134]

1968

These songs, current during the Vietnam conflict are arbitrarily assigned to this, their date-of-publication because none of the texts are dated. These versions and variants were from United States Air Force currency.[135]

The Hamburg Zoo

Barker or leader: Over here, ladies and gentlemen, we have the al-i-ga-tor. Each year the female al-i-ga-tor swims upstream, and lays one million eggs. The male al-i-ga-tor swims upstream and eats 999,999 of those eggs.
Member of the audience: Why does he eat all those eggs?
Barker: Otherwise we'd be up to our ass in al-i-ga-tors.

CHORUS (Repeat after each verse):
Oh, we're off to the Hamburg Zoo,
To see the elephants and the kangaroos,
We'll all be together,
In fair or stormy weather,
We're off to the Hamburg Zoo.

Over here, we have the le-o-pard, the leopard who has one spot for every day of the year. Lift up the le-o-pard's tail and show the lady of the 24th of November. [sic This is probably a sign of mishearing.]

Here we have the tight-skinned owl, whose skin is so tight that every time he blinks he masturbates himself. Little boys have been known to jack him off by throwing sand in his eyes.

Here we have the O-rang-a-tang whose balls hang so low that every time he swings from tree to tree, his balls go O-tang-a-tang.

Over here, ladies and gentlemen, we have the Ki Ki bird. The Ki Ki bird who flies in ever decreasing circles until it flies up its own asshole. The Ki Ki bird can be distinguished by his inimitable cry, "Ki Ki Ki-rist , it's dark in here."

Here we have the Lost Tribes of Africa. The lost tribes of Africa who wandered lost in the jungle for many a year. The lost tribes' cry would be heard in the jungle, "Fuga we, fuga we, where the fug are we,"

The female horny bird can be distinguished by her cry, 'Want some, want some"; and the male horny bird by his cry, "Here it 'tis. Here it 'tis. Here it 'tis."

The Wild West Show II

CHORUS
Ohhh, we're off to see the Wild West Show,
The elephants and the kangaroos,
As long as we're together,
Never mind the weather,
We're off to see the Wild West Show.

Ladies and gentlemen, in this corner we have the _____.
Chorus: Fantastic, incredible, no shit? Tell us about the motherfucker.

Repeat as above, with group interpolation, filling in the blank, followed by the leader's explanation.

The mathematical wonder is a strange girl, indeed.
She was a girl who was ate before she was seven,

The wherethefuckarewe tribe is a very strange tribe indeed.
They are a group of natives who are three feet tall walking around in six feet jungle grass saying, "Where the fuck are we, tribe, where the fuck are we, tribe?"

The oh-no bird makes its home on a corrugated roof.
And the oh-no bird has a two-foot scrotum and one-foot legs. And every time he comes in for a landing, he says, "Ohhhh—no."

Lulu, the tattooed lady, is a very strange lady, indeed.
Lulu, the tattooed lady, has tattooed on one cheek the letter "M,"
And on the other cheek she has tattooed the letter "M";
And when she bends over she says "Mom,"
And she stands on her head, she says, "Wow,"
And when she does cartwheels she says, "Wow, Mom, wow."

Lulu, the tattooed lady's sister, is a very strange woman indeed.
Lulu, the tattooed lady's sister, has tattooed on one thigh "Merry Christmas,"
And on the other thigh she has tattooed "Happy New Year."
And she tells all her friends to come up and see her between the holidays.[136]

1970

The Wild West Show[136]

CHORUS:
We're off to see the Wild West Show,
The elephants and the kangaroo,
Never mind the weather,
As long as we're together,
We're off to see the Wild West Show.

Leader: Step right up, step right up, ladies and gentlemen; in this corner we have the Oh-no-bird.
Group: The Oh-no-bird? What's the Oh-no-bird?

103

Leader: The Oh-no-bird is a bird of the air whose testicles are ten inches longer than the rest of his body and every time he comes in for a landing he can be heard to say: "Oh, No! Oh, No!"

Subsequent verses follow the same call-and-response pattern.

The orangutang is a jungle beast who has two testicles made of solid brass and as he swings from trees he can be heard for miles, "ORANG — UTANG.

The Fuckawi tribe is a tribe of pygmies in central Africa. They roam the savannah grasslands. They are three-feet tall, the grass is four-feet tall. This accounts for why every once in a while you can hear them say, "Where the fuckawi."

The Omatooli bird is a bird whose penis is thirteen inches longer than his body, and as he flies over tall trees he can be heard to say, "Omatooli, omatooli."

The kangaroo is the only animal in the kingdom who finds it culturally permissible to crawl into its mother.

A leopard is an animal with 114 spots. What? You only see 113. Well, lift its tail!

A giraffe is the only animal in the kingdom who can walk into a bar and say, "The high balls are on me."

A tiger is a 400-pound pussy who eats you.

1970
The Wild West Show[137]

CHORUS:
We are off to see the wild west show
With the elephants and the kangaroos.
No matter what the weather, as long as we're together,
We're off to see the wild west show.

Leader: Ladies and gentlemen, in the far ring we have the oo oo aa aa bird.
Group: Oнннн, fantastic, incredible. What the hell is an oo oo aa aa bird?
Leader: The oo oo aa aa bird is a rare and exotic bird found in the deserts of Australia. It has three-foot legs and four-foot testicles, and every time it lands, it goes oo oo aa aa.

Subsequent verses follow the same pattern of call and response followed by the chorus.

The giraffe from the Savannah of Africa is the only animal that can walk into a bar and say, "The highballs are on me."

The wherethefuckarewe tribe is a tribe of four-foot tall pigmies found in deepest, darkest Africa that walks through five-foot high grass shouting, "Where the fuck are we? Where the fuck are we?"

The orangutan bird is found in the mountains of Africa. Its left ball is made of steel and its right ball is made of copper. Every time it lands it goes oran-gu-tan, oran-gu-tan.

The rhinosaurus is reputed to be the richest animal in the world. Its name is derived from the Latin — rhino meaning money and soreass meaning piles. Hence: piles of money.

The kerrii bird lives north of the Arctic Circle. Every time it comes in to land on the ice, it says, "Kerii kerii ker-ist, its cold."

By some strange evolutionary occurrence, the nervous system of the winky wank bird's eyelids are connected to its foreskin. Every time it winks, it wanks, and every time it wanks, it winks.

1971

The Wild West Show[138]

Leader: Ladies and gentlemen, in this corner we have the homosexual spider.

Group: The homosexual spider? FANTASTIC! Incredible. Tell us more about it.

Leader: The homosexual spider instead of catching flies opens them.

CHORUS

1971

"Actually, I now recall a female classmate at NYU, ca. 1971, narrating the bit about the 'Fugawi Indians' as a joke, completely detached from (or not yet attached to) the 'song.'

"As I recall, members of various tribes were sitting around the campfire explaining the origins of their [tribal] names. I don't recall the two 'setup' tribes, but they were appropriately heroic, something like the 'the Buffalo Tribe, because we hunt the mighty buffalo by creeping through the tall grass...' And maybe the Wolf Tribe...' Finally, the Fugawis 'creep through the tall grass, stand up and say...'"[139]

1971

The Wild West Show[140]

Leader: Ladies and gentlemen, in this corner we have the homosexual spider.

Group: The homosexual spider? FANTASTIC! Incredible. Tell us more about it.

Leader: The homosexual spider instead of catching flies opens them.

CHORUS
We are off to see the Wild West show,
The elephants and the kangaroos.
No matter what the weather,
As long as we're together,
We're off to see the Wild West show.

Prior to 1975

In Richard Reuss's files, now deposited in the Indiana University Library, are no fewer than five variants of "The Menagerie" or "Larry's Panorama." All are undated. However, these possibly jury-rigged texts link or fuse "Van Amburgh's Show" (in its "Hamburg Show" derivative), "Menagerie," the *Stag*

Party variant and "The Wild West Show." The first might be a jury-rigged text since Reuss titled it "Larry's Panorama." The linkages or borrowings in the first text are set in italics.

I

In the first cage, ladies and gentlemen, is the wildcat. That native American beast of prey which roams the mountains and the wildernesses of the western Carolinas and Tennessee. It is very closely related to our own tame cat. Now the only difference between the wildcat and the tame cat is that *the wildcat has no asshole; therefore he cannot shit. That's what makes him wild.* Larry, turn the crank.

Reuss wrote a note at the end of the student's contribution: "At the conclusion of each of these speeches, the previous reciter would say, 'Where we goin', boys?' To which the chorus would answer:

CHORUS:
We're going to the Hamburg Show
To see the elephant and wild kangaroo,
And we'll all stick together,
In fair or stormy weather
For we're going to see the whole show through.

The creature in the next cage, ladies and gentlemen, is the tight-skinned monkey from northern India. *This little animal's skin is so tight that every time he winks his eyes, he skins his prick. Now, will the small boys in the front row stop throwing sand at him. This is only a picture.* Larry, turn the crank.

In the next cage is the great cassowary bird, which inhabits the desert vastnesses of central Australia. It is the next largest bird to the ostrick [sic]. One day as the cassowary was roving about in search of his favorite food, the serpent, he spied and uncommonly large and fine one. Hastily bending over *he inguritated the head of the snake, who promptly passed down his throat, the oesophagus, through his stomach, his intestines, and finally wriggled out his asshole.* A second time the snake slipped down his throat, the oesophagus, through his stomach, his intestines, and out his asshole. A third time the cassawary [sic] bent over and

107

swallowed the serpent. Then, turning hurriedly around he thrust his bill up his asshole and cried, triumphantly, "*There, loop the loop, you son of a bitch.*" Larry, turn the crank.

In the next cage, ladies and gentlemen, is the fast-disappearing Rocky Mountain goat. This animal is indigenous to America. He has one very amusing habit in that he jumps lightly from crag to crag, and every time he jumps, he farts. Now, the question before the house is: *"Is it the jump that makes him fart, or the fart that makes him jump."*

In the next picture, ladies and gentlemen, is the world-renowned laughing hyena, inhabiting the African veldt. He is known, from Dan to Beersheba, because he is the laughingest beast that lives. The strange thing about this hyena is that he only has sexual intercourse once every two years. *What the son-of-a-bitch has to laugh about, I don't know.* Larry, turn the crank.

This, ladies and gentlemen, is the far-famed and justly celebrated Fallaloo Bird, which flies backward over the Sahara Desert to keep the sand out of its eyes. It is, as you see, of monstrous size, and if feeds only upon the sands of the Nile. *It is the bird with the rectangular arse-hole — hence the Pyramids.* Larry, turn the crank.

In the next cage, my friends, is exhibited the rarest of all avis, the marvelous and extraordinary Cowah-cowah bird, which lives forever and a day, and dwells solitary and alone upon the highest peak of the Andes. He copulates but one every 99 years, [when] it flies to the lowlands, seeking its mate, and when he finds her, he inveigles her into his den where [he] fucks her, then and there, then wings his majestic way back to his solitary peak, crying in a loud voice, "Co-wah! Co-wah!" which translated into English means: *"I don't get it often, but when I do, Kee-rist!, how I enjoy it."* Larry, turn the crank.

In the next cage, ladies and gentlemen, we see one of the most graceful of the animals of South America. It is the light-footed and beautiful little gazelle which is found only in the inaccessible and precipitous heights of the Chilean Andes. *This little gazelle leaps lightly from precipice to precipice and back to piss again.* Larry, turn the crank.

This, my good people, is the prodigious high-hopping Highbehind, It is a cross between the jackrabbit, the kangaroo and a grasshopper. A full-grown male in good trim and cover two counties, a township, six suburban lots, a brick shit-house and a bull turd at a single bound. He fucks the female on the fly. When reaching the copulative climax, they spin around in the air like a pinwheel, crying "Whoosh! Whoosh! Whoosh!" What is that, sir? How high can the high-hopping Highbehind leap? Why my dear sir, they leap so high that the bluebirds frequently build nests in the Highbehind' arseholes. When this country became so thickly settled that the Highbehinds couldn't hop without landing in a city or town, they all migrated to the moon, making it in eighteen and a half jumps. It rained Highbehind excreta for a week all over North America. ["Larry, turn the crank" is omitted here.]

In the cage on my right is the well-known and justly celebrated spotted leopard. *He has exactly 365 spots*, one for each and every day of the year. What's that, Madam? What does he do in Leap Year? *Boy, lift up the leopard's tail and show the lady the extra spot.* Larry, turn the crank.

In the mahogany case in the center of the tent, fellow scientists, lie the genuine fossilized remains of the extraordinary and almost incredible Whangle-po. The object between his legs looks like a coil of rope, but be not deceived, my good people, it is his penis which he kept wound on a reel, and which was the direct cause of the untimely demise of the species. Thirty eleven squillion years ago, in the Garden of Eden this occurred. For the Whangle-po was created by the Father in a moment of abstraction, and lo and behold, his penis was so long that when he endeavored to copulate, it took him seventy-three weeks to come, and when the charge finally reached the female, she had died of old age, and the pair perished without issue. Larry, turn the crank.

In this picture, folks, we see the mammoth mastodon, the most enormous of all prehistoric beasts. When he was unable to secure the services of the female if the species, he was accustomed to masturbate in the ground. Hence the Mammoth Caves of Kentucky. Larry, turn the crank.

Here we have a marvelously realistic picture of a bird that is now almost extinct — the American ostrich — who, when he is pursued by his enemies, is accustomed *to stick his head in the sand — whereupon he farts through his tail feathers. Hence the trade winds.* Larry, turn the crank.

And now we see the African ostrich, which when pursued by the hunters, runs in a circle. Finding no escape, *it buries its head in the sands of the desert, whistles "God Save the King" through its arse-hole* and claims the protection of the British flag. Larry, turn the crank.

In the next cage will be observed the mighty Rhino-soreass, the richest animal in the jungle. What was that, sir? Why is he the richest animal in the jungle? The answer is obvious. *The word "rhino" is from the ancient Egyptian, meaning money, and soreass is plain old Anglo-Saxon, meaning piles, hence "piles of money."* Larry, turn the crank.

In the last cage, my friends, is the shy and timorous Skigoogus snake. When alarmed out of reach of shelter, *it crawls in its own arse-hole until the danger is past.*

Thank you for your kind attention. Please pass out quietly to your right and don't annoy the animals. Good evening.

II

Ladies and gentlemen, we now come to Livingston in Darkest Africa. Livingston, arriving at a clearing, found all the natives in fete. King Boho, master of them all, [stood] rubbing his enormous talawag to redness, [then hanging from his tool] carried a large calabash full of water about the arena. Livingston, not to be outdone, rubbed HIS enormous talawag to redness likewise, thrust it up the ass of King Boho, and carried not only the calabash but King Boho as well, not once but thrice around the arena to the everlasting glory of the Caucasian race.

This concludes our regular performance but you are earnestly requested to remain for the afterpiece or concert, which will follow immediately. As a marvelous exhibition, ladies and gentlemen, will be shown some rare Oriental masterpieces of art and sculpture stolen from the harem of the Shah of Persia and never previously exhibited in America. As a prelude to this wonderful showing, I present to your notice this beautiful, life-size painting by Rubens, entitled "Faith, Hope and Charity." *I call your particular attention to the Face of Faith, the teats of Hope, and the ass of Charity.* Our gentlemanly ticket agents will now pass among you.

III

Here we have the famous Mexican bird, the Whiffenpoof. This strange bird inhabits the plains of Yucatan, *lives solely upon the succulent Mexican red pepper,* shits chili *and flies backward to keep his asshole cool.* This, my friends, is the night-flying woodpecker, a devilish little bird that flits from house to house, tapping gently on bedroom windows, causing old maids to catch their pussies in both hands and writhe in terror. That is why we have steam laundries.

IV

Ladies and gentlemen, the first chromo for your consideration... On our right we now have the Australian kangaroo. The Australian kangaroo inhabits a barren and stoney plain. Two of these stones he carries with him at all times, thus to propagate his kind.

V

Gentlemen, we now have the picture of the Great American Bear. The Great American Bear inhabits the Cascade Mountains. Fasting through the long hibernation period of winter, he descends the slopes in the springtime ravenously hungry. Entering the Indian villages, *he captures the fairest of the maidens and carries her on high. Then, after much fumbling and fondling, he finally ferociously fucks her.* After which he consumes the carcass, not so much from hunger, mind you, Gentlemen, but to save the poor virgin from shame.

Here we see upon the screen the African Armadillo! *Its skin is so tight that every time he blinks his eye, he skins his prick. The naughty little African boys throw sand in his eyes and watch him jerk himself off.* Larry, turn the crank.

1976

At the top of the first page, Richard Reuss appended this soon to be poignant note: "One of these days I'll get to the study of this song I've been meaning to work up."

The Wild West Show[140]

[All] We're off to see the Wild West Show-oh-oh,
The elephants and the kangar-oo-oos,
Never mind the weather, as long as we're together,
We're off to see the Wild West Show.

[Narrator] And in this corner we have… the African bullfrog.
[Audience]: The African Bullfrog? Fannnnn-tastic? Innnnnnn-credible! What the fuck is the African Bull Frog?
[Narrator] The African Bull Frog, ladies and gentlemen, in that far corner, is a little frog about three inches high.
[Audience] Ohhhhh! Awwwwwh! Three inches high.
[Narrator] But he's got a prick six inches high.
[Audience] Six inches high???
[Narrator] You can hear his call throughout the night: "Rub it, rub it, rub it, rub it."

 Refrain.

Subsequent verses follow the same call-and-response pattern:

Oorang-ootang — This rare ape in the darkest jungles of Africa has two brass testicles. *And as he swings through the trees, all that can be heard is oo-RANG, oo-TANG, oo-RANG, oo-TANG, oo-RANG, oo-TANG.*

Winkie-wackie bird — *The Winkie-wackie is a very rare bird whose foreskin is attached to his eyelids. So, when he winks, he wanks, and when he wanks, he winks.*

The State Rugby Club Pervertable — *The State Rugby Club Pervertable,* owned by the evil Dr. F. Johnson, *is the only vehicle when you can get ate in the front and 69 in the back.*

The Fuckahwee tribe, ladies and gentlemen, is made up of a tribe of (insert name of a short person). They roll around in the grass blades of Wisconsin six feet high, and you can hear their cry throughout the day and night: *"Where the fuck are we? Where the fuck are we? Where the fuck are we?"*

Ladies and gentlemen, in this cage we have the color of the ground of Custer's last stand. The color of the ground of Custer's last stand was white because those Indians kept comin' and comin' and comin' and comin'.

Ladies and gentlemen, in this cage we have the American bald eagle. This rare bird of prey, the finest in the New World, soars at a height of 10,000 feet, and with his sharp eyes he sees a snake wriggling along the ground. He swoops down on the snake, gobbles him up and returns to a height of 10,000 feet. But the snake, being no fool, wriggles through the eagle's esophagus, through his intestines, looks out his anal orifice, and says, "Eagle, how high are we flying?" And the eagle says, "Oh, about 10,000 feet," and the snake says, "You wouldn't shit me, would you, Charlie?"

Ladies and gentlemen, in this corner we have Dean Doyle. Dean Doyle is the only man in the State Rugby Club who has a twelve-inch tongue. And when he takes his girl back at night, he eats her so dry that in the morning she has to prime herself to piss.

Step up, ladies and gentlemen. In this corner we have the Hurricane. Well, there was this guy, he walks into a whorehouse, see. He asks what the day's special is. The lady says it's the Hurricane. He goes, "Okay, I'll take it." Fucker goes upstairs, whore comes up, takes his clothes off, lays down in the bed, squats on his face and farts. He goes, "Fuck, what was that?" She goes, "That was the wind, that was the wind, that was the wind." Then she gets down, bangs his head between her boobs, and he goes, "What was that?" She goes, "That was the thunder, the fuckin' thunder, man, the thunder." And then she gets down and squats down on his face and pisses all over him. She goes, "That was the rain, that was the rain." He gets up and says, "Shit!" puts on his clothes, walks outside. She goes,

"What's a matter?" He goes, "Aw, I can't fuck in this kinda weather."

1978

This version was collected by Ron Edwards from Allen Holmes (born in 1890) then living in Theodore, Queensland, on May 15, 1978, and published in *The Australian Folklore Society Journal* Number 21 (January, 1993).[141] The text below is copied verbatim from Edwards' notes.

The Showman

1. Here we have the Dromedary, "the ship of the desert," what eats sand and shits bricks. It has a triangular asshole, hence the Pyramids.
2. This, ladies and gentlemen, is the hippopotamus, derived from the Latin words hippo (float) and pottamous (bottoms upwards), and this is the position in which it copulates — hence the rise and fall of the Nile.
3. This animal, ladies and gets [sic, for gents] is the Rhinosaurarse, derived from the two Latin words, rhino (indicating money or pelf) surarsse [sic] (a very delicate allusion to piles). This uroesus [sic] of an animal has a hide so tough that no weapon can penetrate it. How then is it killed? The natives of the jungle foregather in large crowds, track it to its lair, rouse it with loud cries and much beating of Tom-Toms, off it goes, up goes its tail, and in speeds the fatal arrow.
4. This is the Ourang-Ourang. What is strange among these animals is that they copulate belly-to-belly, just the same as you and I do, lady. And enjoy it just as much.
5. This, ladies and gents, is the Comfah bird, what is found in the mountains of Greece. Its staple food is cayenne pepper, and it has to fly backwards to keep his arse cool.
6. This is the Chimpanzee, or man monkey, who gets down from the mountain fastnesses into the villages. He carries off the maidens to his lair and there he fondles, fumbles and finally rapes them, muttering at the same time "ayar ayar" what interpreted means "good, bloody good". He then devours the victim of his lust, thus covering the traces of his crime and at the same time conserving his seed.
7. This, ladies and gents, is the Flamingo or Red Bird. Its wings are red, its beak is red, his feet is [sic] red and its shit is red — hence the

anchovy paste of commerce, what is found on the tables of the upper classes.

8. Here we have the Chamois, or Mountain Goat what jumps from precipice to precipice and back to piss. He farts when he jumps and vice-versa, but as Professor Huxley maintains, we have no data to determine whether he farts because he jumps or jumps because farts.
9. This is the laughing hyena, which belies his name, in as much as he cannot shit, and can do the naughty once a year; and what the hell he has to laugh at I don't know.
10. Under the microscope, we see the smallest thing in nature, to wit, Nits on a Gnat's nuts.
11. And then we have the Ostrich, found on the sandy deserts of Af-ry-ka. Why is he so hard to catch? When the hunters are close up to him he has a habit of sticking his beak in the sand and laughs in the face of his bitter pursuers, and this, my friends, accounts for the milk in the cocoanut [sic].
12. This is the Spotted Leopard, from central Af-ry-ka. It has 365 spots, one for every day of the year. What did you say, Lady? Leap year? Horace, lift up his tail and show the lady the 29th of February.
13. This, ladies and gents, is the Marmoset. Horace, remove the lemonade bottle from his whatsit. While not wishing to interfere with his innocent pleasure, we must uphold the morality of the show.
14. And now, my friends, I must ask all little boys and girls, and those not able to swim, to please leave the tent, because the elephant is about to make water.

1979

The Wild West Show[142]

CHORUS:
Oh, we're off to see the Wild West Show,
The elephant and the Kangaroo,
Never mind the weather,
As long as we're together,
We're off to see the Wild West Show.

Now, here, ladies and gentlemen, in the first cage we have the laughing hyena. This animal lives in the mountains and once every year comes down to eat. Once every two years he comes down to drink and once every three years he comes down for sexual intercourse. What the ****** [goddam] hell he has to laugh about, I don't know.

And in the next cage we have the giraffe. This creature is the most popular animal in the animal kingdom. Why? Every time he goes into a bar he says: "The highballs are on me."

And here, ladies and gentlemen, we have the Orangutang. As this animal proceeds from branch to branch, swinging through the forest, his balls orang-u-tang, orang-u-tang.

And in the next cage we have the Oster-reich. This animal, at the first sign of danger, buries is head in the sand and whistles through the whole of the afternoon.

And in the next cage we have the Rhinoceros. This animal is reputed to be the richest in the world. Its name is derived from the Latin — rhino meaning money and sore **** [arse] meaning piles, hence piles of money.

And here we have the keerie bird. This bird lives in the Antarctica. And every time it comes in to land on the ice, [it] says "Keerie, keerie, kerr-ist it's cold."

And in this cage we have the Winky Wankee Bird. By some strange happening, the nervous system of this bird's eyelids is connected to its foreskin. Every time it winks, it wanks and every time it wanks, it winks. You, boy, stop throwing sand in the bird's eyes.

And here is the elephant. The elephant has a ginormous [sic] appetite. In one day it eats two tons of hay, one dozen bunches of bananas and twenty buckets of rice. Madam, don't stand to near the elephant's backside. Madam — Madam! Too late. George, dig her out.

And here, ladies and gentlemen, we have the Oozle Woozle Bird. These birds fly in a line ahead formation, and at the first sign of danger, the last bird flies up the **** [arse] of the bird in front and so on up the line. The remaining bird flies around in ever decreasing circles, finally disappearing up its own orifice from which position it proceeds to shower **** [shit] and derisions in all directions.

ca 1982

The Wild West Show[143]

CHORUS:
We're off to see the Wild West Show
The elephants and the kangaroos
Whenever we're together
There's never stormy weather
We're off to see the Wild West Show.

Leader: Step right up and see the amazing (insert animal's name)!
Crowd: The amazing (insert animal's name)!
Leader: Yes, the amazing (insert animal's name)!
Crowd: FANTASTIC!, INCREDIBLE!, NO SHIT! Tell us about the motherfucker!
Leader: names the animal.

> The Oh No Bird is an amazing little bird. Its legs are three inches long and its balls are twelve inches long. Whenever he comes in for a landing, he goes, "Oh, No! Oh, No!"

> The Milormor Bird. He is a cousin of the Oh No Bird. He also has three inch legs and twelve inch balls. And when he comes in for a landing you can hear him for a mile or more.

> Rat-A-Tat Bird. He is another cousin of the Oh No Bird. He also has three inch legs and twelve inch balls. He always lands on railroad tracks. When he comes in for a landing he goes, "Rat-a-tat-tat, Rat-a-tat-tat."

> The Kiki Bird. The Kiki Bird is a little bird who lives on the South Pole and when it's real cold at night you can hear his cry, "Ki, Ki, Ki-rist, it's cold!"

The Wicky-Wacky Bird. His foreskin is attached to his eyelid. When he wacks, he winks, and when he winks, he wacks. [sic] (DON'T THROW SAND IN HIS EYE, LADY!)

The Tattooed Lady. The Tattooed Lady has a "W" tattooed on her left cheek of her ass and another "W" tattooed on the right cheek of her ass. When she stands up it says "WOW", when she stands on her head it says, "MOM," and when she does cartwheels it says, "WOW, MOM"!

The Tattooed Lady's Sister. The Tattooed Lady's Sister has "Merry Christmas" tattooed on the inside of her right thigh and "Happy New Year" tattooed on the inside of her left thigh. She always says, "Stop up and see me between the holidays."

The Mathematical Impossibility. There she is, the Mathematical Impossibility, the only woman who was "eight" before she was seven.

The Amazing American Station Wagon. The Amazing American Station Wagon is the only automobile in the world where you can get "eight" in the front and sixty-nine in the back.

The Bengal Tiger. The Bengal Tiger is the only pussy in the world that is so big, it eats you.

The Orangutan. The Orangutan is a jungle creature with brass balls, and as he swings through the trees you can hear them go, Or-ang-u-tang, Or-ang-u-tang!

The Laid Back Rhino. The Laid Back Rhino is a creature that no matter how many times he gets laid, he's still horny.

The Pornographic Woodland Creatures. The Pornographic Woodland Creatures number in the thousands, and include the two legged dear, the bear assed bear [bore?], the one eyed winking worm, the horny toad, the zipper snake, the trouser trout, and the wide open beaver.

The Fugawi Tribe. The Fugawi Tribe is a group of African natives. They stand four-foot tall and live in grass that is six feet high. All day long they keep jumping up and down saying, "We ['re] the Fugawi!, We ['re] the Fugawi!"

The Moanback Tribe. The Moanback Tribe is another group of African natives. They are commonly found behind garage trucks saying, "Mon back, Mon back." ["Come on back, come on back"]

The Ho-Di-Do Tribe. The Ho-Di-Do Tribe is another group of African natives commonly found running for an elevator yelling, "Ho de do, Man."[144]

The Pigmy Rapist. The Pigmy Rapist is a little fucker about this tall.

The Navy Ensign. He takes out gorgeous women. He wines them and dines them. He dances them and romances them. And at the end of the evening, he's cuddling her on her front door step and he says, "How about a little good night fuck?" And she replies, "Good night, fuck!"

The Navy Lieutenant. He only dates bi-sexuals. He wines them and dines them. He dances them and romances them. And at the end of the evening, he's cuddling her on her front doorstep and he says, "How about a little sex?" And she replies, "Bye!"

The Navy Commander. Let me tell you about the Navy Commander. I met him in a bar one night. He was sitting there with ten martinis in front of him. I said, "Why do you have ten martinis in front of you?" To which he replied, "I am celebrating my first blow job." I asked if I could buy him another one and he said, "No, if ten don't get the taste out of my mouth, nothing will."

The Navy Captain. Let me tell you about the Navy Captain. I met him in a bar one night. He was sitting there with ten martinis in front of him. I said, "Why do you have ten martinis in front of you?" To which he replied, "I am celebrating my first fuck." I asked him if I could buy him another one and he said, "No, if ten don't kill the pain in my ass, nothing will."

1985

This partial text of "The Wild West Show" is from the 1985 version of the 43rd Tactical Squadron's songbook compiled by Paul Woodford and the late Charles "Zippy" Baumerich. It is worth printing in part for the first verse that demonstrates adaptation to U.S. Air Force currency.

"Good evening, ladies and gentlemen. Welcome to the Wild West Show."

> Chorus:
> Oh, we're off to see the Wild West Show,
> The elephants and the kangaroos.
> No matter what the weather, as long as we're together
> We're off to see the Wild West Show.

> Intro: "Tonight for you we have the most fantastic, incredible animal acts ever seen before the eyes of man of the face of this earth. Tonight for you we have the famous Ki-Ki-Ki-Ki bird.
> Audience: "Fantastic, incredible, tell us about the motherfucker!"
> The Ki-Ki-Ki-Ki Bird is a very strange animal indeed. He flies along at 21,500 looking for targets. As he spies his prey, he folds his wings and starts down a precise 75-degree dive. Down he goes gaining speed — 18,000', 10,000' — His vision begins to blur from the wind blast — 7,000' — faster and faster — 3,000' — 1,500' — 500' — He starts his pull out — 100' — 50' — He puts out his wings, grabs his prey with his mighty talons and says "Ki, Ki, Ki, Krist that was close!"

1990s

"We used to sing the song in the days when I was in the Army Cadet Force at my Grammar School in Grimsby, Lincolnshire, UK where it was known as "The Wild West Show." Verses I recall include "The Umagooly Bird," "The Fuckawe Tribe," and "The Winky-Wanky Bird."[145]

1995

Among U.S. Navy SEALs in training, "As we started toward the instructor's sea-hut, we began singing an old team ditty:

"We're off to see the Wild West Show,
The elephants and the kangaroos
As long as we're together,
We'll never fear the weather
We're off to see the Wild West Show.

Ladies and gentlemen,
In this corner is the incredible Orang-u-tang!"[146]

2003

MP3 downloaded by Paul Stamler of St. Louis reportedly sung by John Roberts and Tony Barrand. Stamler also noted this corporate internet site: www.fugawi.com. The company sells global positioning satellite software.

2004

At the request of coauthor John Patrick, forty-four people replied to Patrick's appeal for additional verses. The majority of those responding were British.

Georgiansilver wrote, "I used to sing it with the lads on the rugby coach:

[Barker:] In this cage, ladies and gentlemen, we have the red pepper bird.
Group: The red pepper bird! What the [fuckin]g hell is that?
[Barker:] The red pepper bird eats red pepper, drinks red pepper, and flies
    backwards to keep its a[ss] cool.

A guest, Hootenanny, replied. "Used to sing this at school and into my teens. From the printed verses above you seem to have omitted the Pie Bird, the one with the triangular arse hole that flies across the desert shitting pyramids. Hootenanny added, "If memory serves me right, the introduction started with a recitation something like:

"Roll up, ladies, roll up, gents
See the greatest show in tents
See the leopard's 100 spots
Ninety-nine on his back and one on his
Cock your eyes over here, folks, etc. etc."

Emma B. contributed a comment: She had not sung the song "since school "charabanc" trips — but brings back memories."

Tony "learned long ago from boat club and rugby club associates:

> "And in this tank, ladies and gentlemen, we have the shark. The shark is the most voracious feeder in the seas. It eats seal, fish and the occasional passing swimmer. What was that, lady? Does it swallow yer 'ole? Nah, it spits it out when it comes to it."

> "And in this cage we have the ozzle-woozle bird. These birds fly in a single line with the largest bird in front, followed by the next largest and so on down to the smallest at the rear. At the first sign of danger, the smallest bird flies up the behind of the bird in front and so on up the line. The single remaining bird then flies round and round in ever decreasing circles until it disappears up its own fundamental orifice, from which advantageous position to proceeds to shower shit and derision in all directions."

Someone signing on as the Walrus noted, "The 'end of the show' was usually signalled by the group 'leader' (or some member, having got bored by the whole performance) announcing: "And now, will all you small children please get into the boat. The elephant is about to piss."

Leadfingers suggested, "This is one of those songs that ONLY works with audience participation — IF you can get the 'people' to add their own verses…"

Steve Parkes wrote, "The pygmy verse works particularly well in the West Midlands where 'where' is pronounced 'weer'. [This would suggest that Gershon Legman is rather premature in his judgment that the cante-fable is of Australian origin.] In polite circles they are known as the Ellawi tribe." He continued, "The leopard, according to my little brother, goes: 'The spotted leo-pard has one spot for every day of the year. What's that, madam? Leap years? George, lift the le-o-pard's tail and show the lady the 29th of February.'"

Major Matt Mason learned "The Wild West Show" "from my Da thirty years ago here in the States. He always sang it with a Cockney accent."

And now we have the Oo-Ah Bird!
Audience: The Oo-Ah Bird! Fan-TASTIC!
The Oo-Ah Bird lays square eggs with sharp corners, and can be recognized by his distinctive cry, "OOOOOOO-AHHHHHHHH!"

Dennis Malone pointed out "when I played rugby at Iowa in '71–72, the verse I remember was:

> In this corner, ladies and gentlemen (as if there were any ladies) we have the fantastic and amazing KIWI bird. This is the only bird in the whole wide world that actually eats roots, shoots and leaves! We are off to see the wild west show!

Charles Kratz learned the song from a young woman who was working at Timberline Lodge on Mt. Hood in Oregon. "I added a verse about the bodini bird which took off from the Amazon jungle in great flocks and flew single file in ever decreasing circles at ever increasing speed until each bird flew his head up the arse of the bird ahead of him, and at this time, all gave out their beautiful mating call, 'I — CAN'T — SEE — FOR — SHIT!"

Edthefolkie notes the chorus was sung, but the animals were presented "in a loud voice like a fairground barker." He added, "Learned some of it while in the Combined Cadet Force of a supposedly respectable UK public day school. We used to sing it on the bus on the way back from a wooded area where we rushed about like Dad's Army or that of Fred Karno. Obviously a hangover from HM Forces, National Service backwards to WW II and WW I."

Bryn Pugh offered "another aside re: the WinkiWanki Bird: This species is rapidly becoming extinct because small boys throw sand in its eyes. But it dies with a smile in its face. Ernie — turn the fuckin' crank!"

An unidentified guest, who learned the song in his local pub, wrote of the Fu-Fu bird, "Now ladies and gentlemen, this bird soars 2,000 feet in the sky and swoops down to within two inches of the ground and the way back up he goes, [crying] "Fu-fu-fuck, that was close!"

Rowan, writing from Melbourne, cited the triangular asshole bird, which eats only sand and can shit only every few millennia. The first times it produced the pyramids, and most recently it produced the YMCA. (He explained that the symbol for the Y was, in the early 1960's, a triangle and, in Melbourne, the building was triangular in plan.)

Also from the same era and location: "And in this cage, ladies and gentlemen, we have the cryptic church mouse, Very discreet, it crept into the crypt, crapped and crept out again."

An unidentified guest contributed: "Ladies and gentlemen, here we have the ostrich. (Group): The ostrich? (Leader) Yes, the ostrich. This amazing bird, ladies and gentlemen, can not only not fly, but it lays eggs so large that every time it lays one, its ass stretches."

Another guest offered, "In this corner we have the Zebra. It's the only creature in the whole wide world that is 26 sizes bigger than an A bra."

And this, as well: "In this corner, we have a porcupine, a very strange creature indeed. It is the only creature with 1000 pricks, and no, Ms. Jones, he is not for sale."

Eliza, a guest, added a couple of sociological observations: "My first boyfriend taught me this in Edinburgh in 1968. I thought he was wonderful, but he had to explain several of the verses. He always sang the chorus, and *narrated the verses in a pseudo-American accent*. (Emphasis added.) He also taught me about a man who had "large balls, twice as heavy as lead" who apparently "with a singular twist of his muscular wrist, he threw them over his head" ["Do Your Balls Hang Low?"] Does anyone know that one? I was only seventeen and completely innocent and naive. I smile now; I was horrified and fascinated in equal measure! He is now professor of epidemiology in Scotland. I don't suppose he sings this song any more!"

Threelegsoman added that "as a young man at college, I used to sing this song in coach trips returning from hockey matches." "Guest" noted, "I learned what I still consider one of the cleverest verses at the knee of my older cousin, an FP of George Heriot's Edinburgh, whom ne'er a school surpasses for bawdy songs and their hit verses. Any part of its phraseology that may not be quite English as she ought to be spoke, does however reflect the way things are expressed in Scotia's genteel capital. (Alba gu bràth!)

> [Barker:] And in the next cage, ladies and gentlemen, we have the POLAR BEAR!
> Group: Charles fucking Darwin! What the hell is that?
> Barker: The polar bear, ladies and gentlemen, lives on an iceberg near the North Pole. On one side of the iceberg there is a Frenchman who keeps a private school and on the other side of the iceberg there is an Italian who keeps a private school. And all day long the polar bear skites (skates?) back and forth on its arse between them keeping its privates cool.

2011

"...[T]his theme is still widely sung in the UK at their [rugby] social gatherings."[147]

2011

Additional verses will be found at Paul Woodford, known in Hash House Harrier circles as "Flying Booger," at his online songbook. Woodward's version adds more audience participation in that each verse is sung by a different member of "the pack."

The Wild West Show[148]

CHORUS:
We're off to see the Wild West Show.
The elephant and the kangaroo-oo-oo,
Never mind the weather, as long as we're together,
We're off to see the Wild West Show.

Leader: Now here, ladies and gentlemen, we have the Oster-reich.
Pack: The oster-reich? Fantastic! Incredible! What the fuck is an oster-reich? Tell us about the son-of-a-bitch.
Leader: This animal, at the first sign of danger, buries its head in the sand and whistles through the 'hole of the afternoon.

Leader: Here, ladies and gentlemen, we have a tattooed lady. On one leg she has tattooed "Fire," and on the other leg she has tattooed "Brimstone," and in between it looks like hell.

Leader: Next we have the French Pervertible. This fine automobile is the last of its kind, no longer for sale anywhere in the world. Notice the convertible top, the five-speed manual transmission, the automatic cruise control, and the dual halogen headlights. It seats two in the front and comfortably accommodates 69 in the back.

Leader: The antique sales lady. The antique sales lady sells only period furniture… everything has stains on it.

Leader: The female mathematician. This lady, folks, believes that this (holding fingers spread about three inches apart) is twelve inches.

Leader: The homosexual sparrow. This bird is so-called, ladies and gentlemen, because he sometimes flies backwards for a lark.

2011

The site of the following extracts of the "Wild West Show," www.hashing.com/songs, has since been taken down and apparently is no longer available. It too begins with the familiar chorus, "We're off to see the Wild West Show," but includes these unusual or unique verses:

The El-e-phant has an enormous appetite. In one day it eats two tons of hay, one dozen bunches of bananas and twenty buckets of rice. Madam, please don't stand too near the elephant. Madam? Madam? Oh, dear God! George, get the shovel.

The second tattooed lady. On one leg she has tattooed "Fire" and on the other leg she has tattooed "Brimstone" and in between it looks like Hell!

The gay-zelle. This pretty, little, four-footed animal you see on your right, ladies and gentlemen, wot has the peculiarity that every time it leaps from rock to rock it farts, and the scientists are still trying to determine whether it farts because it leaps or whether it leaps because it farts.

The Plumb Line Bird. This bird spends most of its time high above the world's oceans, circling in the jet stream until it spies what it is after. Immediately it folds its wings, dives towards the sea, and gathers an ever increasing momentum until it reaches terminal velocity. At that precise moment, it hits the surface of the sea but continues diving straight down, now with decreasing momentum, until, if it has got the timing precisely right, it comes to a stop behind a sardine which has just farted, whereupon it seizes the bubble in its beak for use in spirit levels.

The Triangular Iceberg. A most uncommon iceberg, ladies and gentlemen, where on the first side you will see an Indonesian keeping a private school, and on the second side an American keeping a private school, while on the third side you will see a polar bear sliding up and down, keeping his privates cool.

2012

Retrieved on January 18, 2012 as posted on rugbysongs.net, No. 145, was the following naval (?) version:

Ladies and gentlemen, in this corner we have the admiral's daughter. Yes, the admiral's infamous daughter. She is the final resting place for discharged semen.

Ladies and gentlemen, in this corner we have the ch-ch-Christ Bird. This bird has one wing half as long as the other. Thus it flies in ever decreasing concentric circles, until it flies up its own anal orifices, and then shouts, "Ch-Ch-Christ, it's dark in here!"

As posted, this version has the standard "as long as we're together" chorus.

2012

These unusual verses, in English, were accessed from a site in the Netherlands: www.erc69.nl/song/wild-west-show/

And in the next cage we have the pi-bald pony.
This is a strange, very small animal because it has
Balls which are exactly 3.14159 inches big.

The last animal of the show, ladies and gentlemen,
We have the Bye-bye bird.
The Bye-bye bird sits on the gate
And every time someone leaves, it says, "Oh, piss off."

ENDNOTES

1. Despite the following disclaimers, the sole author and responsible party for this twisted tale is Ed Cray.

2. Richard A. Reuss (1940–1986) and the author of this monograph in approximately 1970 quite independently began work on the life and times of the commonly known bawdy rugby song entitled "The Wild West Show." Another career beckoning, Cray deferred to Reuss, whose academic career, unfortunately, was cut short after he received his doctorate in 1971. Though he taught folklore at his alma mater, Indiana University; at UCLA, Wayne State, and the University of Michigan, tenure in folklore studies eluded him. With his death from complications from respiratory disease, his widow, Joanne, turned over to Indiana University's library her husband's accumulated files. Because so many of the texts in this monograph were found in the Reuss files, it seemed appropriate to posthumously cite him as a co-author.

3. John Patrick, an adept at online research, similarly deserves co-authorship for his indefatigable efforts to retrieve, quite unbidden, via the Internet, versions and variants of the later root song, "The Wild West Show." Without Patrick's contributions, this would have been a much shorter and less authoritative monograph.

4. Francis Teague, *The Curious History of Bartholomew Fair* (Lewisburg: Bucknell University Press, 1985), p. 13.

5. Henry Morley, *Memoirs of Bartholomew Fair*, rep. edn (London: Hugh Evelyn, 1973, reprinting the first edition: London; Chapman and Hall, 1859), p. 148.

6. www.anobii.com/books/Bartholomew_Fair/.../00dd1501e1a7dcb817/

7. Morley, p. 149.

8. Teague, p. 36.

9. The melody, known more popularly as "Packington's Pound," will be found in William Chappell's *Popular Music of the Olden Time*, rep. edn, Vol. I (London: Chappell and Co., 1859; New York, Dover Publications, 1965), p. 123. The full text of "A Caveat for Cutpurses," as set to "Packington's Pound," is in William Chappell, *The Roxburghe Ballads*, vol. III, Printed for the Ballad Society (London: Stephen Austin and Sons, 1875), p. 492–93. In the play Jonson deliberately links broadside sellers with cutpurses or pickpockets.

10. Quoted by Teague, p. 66, from the Pepys diary, edited by Robert Latham, William Matthews et al. (Berkeley: University of California Press, 1970), Vol. II, pp.116–17. See also Teague, p. 68.

11. Morley, p. 229.

12. Teague, p. 79.

13. Teague, p. 93.

14. Teague, p. 89.

15. William B. Boulton, *The Amusements of Old London* (London: John C. Nimmo, 1901), p. 43. The fair itself, first authorized by Henry I in 1133, ran virtually uninterrupted until 1855. Originally intended as a market for drapers and cloth merchants, by the time of good Queen Bess the merchants had moved elsewhere and the three-day fair had mutated into a fourteen-day saturnalia. (Well before then, it had also attracted a procession of married women and widows of all classes — and all masked — to repair for diversion and dalliance to the "Cloisters" of the former church dedicated to St. Bartholomew.)

16. Boulton, pp. 54–56. The first menagerie to appear at Bartholomew's Fair came to London-town about 1650. Morley rescued a handbill that boasted: "Now to be seen or sold, from the end of Hosier Lane, during Bartholomew Fair, a large and beautiful young camel, from Grand Cairo in Egypt. This creature is twenty-three years old; his head and neck are like those of a deer." See also Morley, p. 230.

17. Teague, p. 104.

18. Boulton, p. 57. This is an oblique reference to Issac Van Amburgh.

19. This section of Wordsworth's *The Prelude* is quoted by Teague on page 105. It was first published in 1805 and, again, after Wordsworth's death, in 1850.

20. See Legman's *The Horn Book* (New Hyde Park, New York: University Books, 1964), p. 372.

21. G. Legman, *Rationale of the Dirty Joke*, (New York: Grove Press, 1968), p. 300.

22. *Southern Folklore Quarterly*, Vol. 40 (1976), pp. 64–69.

23. Legman to Reuss, July 21, 1975. Quoted with the kind permission of Ms. Judith Legman and the cooperation of Ms. Joanne Reuss.

24. Matthews' first name is cited in Russell Sanjek, *American Popular Music Business from 1790 to 1909*, Vol. II (Oxford University Press, 1988), pp. 157–58. Matthews' song was apparently first printed in *The Hibernian Cabinet: A Section of all the Most Popular Irish Songs* (London: Printed for T. Hughes, Ludgate Street, 1817). Ten years later, an abridged version was printed in *The British Minstrel and National Melodist*, Vol. I (London: Sherwood, Gilbert and Piper, Paternaster Row, 1827), pp. 279–84.

25. Jonathan Lighter, editor of the *Random House Historical Dictionary of American Slang* which will be concluded by Oxford University Press, in a personal email to Cray suggested that "blue" is an intensifier, that quick-footed Rolla is, in fact, warning those at the fair.

26. Matthews returned to London and the Adelphi Theatre with "Humours of a Country Fair" published in *The Melodist and Mirthful Olio*, Vol. IV, No. 49 (Printed and published by H. Arliss, 35 Gutter Lane, Cheapside, 1829) and again in the following year in *The Apollo, A Collection of the Most Popular Songs, Recitations, Duets*, (London: H. Arliss, now giving his address as Addle Street, Wood Street, Cheapside), Vol. II, p. 25.

27. Doctor W.J. Wetmore's "Van Amburghs [sic] Menagerie" was published by D.S. Holmes of Brooklyn, and dated to 1865. It was retrieved on July 7, 2011 from https: jschol-

arship.library.jhu.edu/bitstream/handle/1774.2 on July 7, 2011. American reprints, all without credit to Wetmore, include *Bob Hart's Planation Songster* (New York: Robert M. Dick and Fitzgerald, 1870?), pp. 63–64; *The Old Clown's "W-h-o-a, January" Songster* (New York: Robert M. De Witt), pp. 6–7; and *The Beauty of the Blondes' Songster* (New York: Dick and Fitzgerald, 1870). The tentative dates of the songsters are given in Norm Cohen, *American Secular Songsters* (Murfreesboro, Tennessee: Middle Tennessee State University, 2000, 2400), pp. 32 ff.

28. The text and tune for "The Royal Wild Beast Show" were furnished by Dick Gardham (Gardhams@Hotmail.com) on October, 1, 2003. The text is by Frank W. Green, the music by Alfred Lee. It was apparently published in an anthology entitled *The Original Christy's Minstrels* by C. Sheard, of 192 High Holborn. The date of publication is unknown; Gardhams tentatively dates it to 1860.

29. C.T. Miller's "The Menagerie" is included in Henry Randall Waite's *Carmina Collegensia: A Complete Collection of the Song of the American Colleges* (Boston: Oliver Ditson, 1876), pp. 90–93.

30. Jonathan Lighter, editor of the *Historical Dictionary of American Slang*, in a private communication with the author, has defined the phrase "over the left" as a negative. It is apparently somewhat less emphatic than the contemporary negative, "like hell."

31. This is the first appearance in what has come to be known as the raree-show (rarity) tradition. It seemingly first appeared in Alfred P. Burbank, ed., *A Collection of Humorous, Dramatic and Dialect Selections* (New York: Dick and Fitzgerald, Publishers, 1878), pp. 44–46.

32. William C. Smith, *Queen City Yesterdays: Sketches of Cincinnati in the Eighties*, rep. edn (Crawfordsville, Ind: R.E. Banta, 1959), p. 41.

33. *The Stag Party* (n.p., n.d.) but said to be printed in Detroit between 1884 and 1890. If Field (1850–1895) is to be credited, he moved to Chicago as a reporter for the *Daily News* in 1883, then perhaps Chicago would be the city of origin.

34. *Actionable Offenses: Indecent Phonograph Recordings from the 1890s* (Champaign, Illinois: Archeophone 1007, 2007), Track 13, "Michael Casey Exhibiting His Panorama." Eric Nizum's liner notes advise that "nineteenth century audiences would have understood that Casey is exhibiting a 'moving panorama,' a series of artworks on a long canvas mounted on two spools."

35. As printed in *The Aurora* (Michigan State Normal College, Yipsilanti, 1908) Vol. XV, p. 206.

36. The Mencken quote is courtesy of Jonathan Lighter, editor of an *Historical Dictionary of American Slang*, the remaining volumes of which are to be published by Oxford University Press.

37. Claude Simpson, *The British Broadside Ballad and Its Music* (New Brunswick, N.J.: Rutgers University Press, 1966), pp. 615–16. For other appearances of the tune,

see too William Chappell, *The Ballad Literature and Popular Music of the Olden Time* (New York: Dover Publications, 1965), Vol. I, pp. 322–23. Hyder E. Rollins, *An Analytical Index of the Ballad Entries (1557–1709)*, reprint edition, (Hatboro, Pennsylvania: Tradition Press), p. 201, lists "Rome for Companie in Bartholomew faire," which may be the same. When dealing with broadsides, Rollins notes in his preface to *A Pepysian Garland*, (Cambridge, Mass.: Harvard University Press, 1922, 1971), p. xi, "Ballads were not written for poetry. They were, in the main, the equivalent of modern newspapers… Journalistic ballads outnumbered all over types."

38. This text and tune were retrieved from Mudcat.org as "Room for Company." "Broom-men" are those who, for tips, sweep ordure from the path of those among the gentry who wish to cross streets. As defined by the *Shorter Oxford English Dictionary*, "botchers" are menders, especially cobblers or tailors. "Paviers," or more properly, "paviours," are those who lay paving stones. "Pinners" are those who impound stray animals. "Pointers" are masons who use strong mortar to seal brickwork. ("Pointers" might also refer to women who tat lacework, but those women would be the only occupation on this otherwise all-male list of cuckolds.) Sailmen are sailmakers; horse-coursers are those who job horses in large lots while farriers are men who shoe horses and treat horses' ailments. A carver is "one who carves wood, ivory or stone," that is, a sculptor. A fellmonger is a dealer in skins and hides, especially those of sheep. Bowyers are those who make, or trade in bows [that shoot arrows]. Drawers may be tapsters, or one who drafts a legal document, or a draftsman, or, simply, one who draws. All are men including "punks" or procurers, as defined in J.S. Farmer and W. E. Henley, *Slang and Its Analogues*, Vol. V.

39. Hyder E. Rollins, *An Analytical Index to the Ballad-Entries (1557–1709) in the Registers of the Company of Stationers of London*, Reprint Edition, (University of North Carolina Press, 1924; Hatboro, Pennsylvania: Tradition Press, 1967), p. 201, No. 2324. Rollins at Nos. 164 and 165 cites "A Bartholomew Fairing" licensed to Richard Harper on September 23, 1639, which begins "You Bartholomew tapsters I first do advise." Continuing the satirical lineage, in 1701 R. Hine was issued a license to publish "A Walk to Smithfield, or a True Description of the Humours of Bartholomew Fair, with the very comical Intrigues and Frolics that are acted in every particular Booth in the Fair…" See *Eighteenth Century Collections Online, Printed for R. Hine*, Gale Publications, Document number CW33079336706. An emasculated paraphrase is in Morley, pp. 351–353.

40. Morley's *Memoirs of Bartholomew Fair*, p. 240.

41. Morley, p. 242–43.

42. Morley, pp. 244–45. See also p. 246–248.

43. Lowest house: Morley, p. 254.

44. Morley, quotes *Wit and Drollery: Jovial Poems* (dated to 1682) on p. 288; with such errata as "woman" for "whore." See the "The Humours of Bartholomew Fair" in

Edward F. Rumbault, *A Little Book of Songs and Ballads* (London: John Russell Smith, 1859), pp. 160–61.

45. Edward F. Rimbault, *A Little Book of Songs and Ballads* (London: John Russell Smith, 1859), p. 166–169. (Compare this with the entry for the year 1682.) The same song is in Morley, p. 249, as "Roger in Amaze, or The Countryman's Ramble Through Bartholomew Fair" and in Thomas D'Urfey, *Pills to Purge Melancholy*, in both the editions of 1707 (Vol. I, p. 55) and 1719–20 (Vol. III, p. 41–43). In all, Rimbault, pp. 160–69, reprints four songs relating to the fair, its humours and its heroes.

46. In the Hebrew *Book of Judith*, the widow Judith beheads the drunken Holofernes, the commander of an invading Assyrian army. Ostensibly, this show — and the others cited — was a panorama depicting the climactic moment. This *may* be the first hint of a stereopticon-like show.

47. Rimbault, *Little Book*, p. 163, footnote.

48. Quoted in Morley, pp. 289–90.

49. Rimbault, pp. 160–61, adds in a footnote to this song crediting "a printed bill of the latter end of the seventeenth century, where it is stated that 'at Crawley's show, at the Golden Lion, near St. George's Church, during the time of Southwark Fair, will be presented the whole Story of the old Creation of the World, or Paradice [sic] Lost, yet newly reviv'd, with the addition of Noah's flood.'" Rimbault adds that he possesses a license on vellum with the seal of the Master of the Revels, dated 1662 permitting George Bayley, of London, Musitioner [sic, for musician] to make show of a play, called *Noah's Flood*. Rimbault also cites a handbill that begins: *"By Her Majesties [sic] Permission.* At Heatly's booth, over against the crossed daggers, next to Mr. Miller's booth, during the time of Bartholomew Fair, will be presented a little Opera, called *The old Creation of World,*, newly reviv'd, with the addition of the glorious battle obtained over the French and Spanish, by his Grace the Duke of Marlborough...." That would date the handbill sometime after August 13, 1704, and the battle of Blenheim in the War of Spanish Succession.

50. Rimbault, p. 162. "Raffling" in the text refers to casting dice, or some other game of chance. "Pise," meaning a method of construction using clay and rock, makes little sense here. In a footnote on this page, Rimbault suggests that the arrival of Punch and Judy shows to Great Britain may have occurred as early as 1660.

51. Steve Roud has indexed a broadside with that title in the Madden Collection microfilmed for the Vaughn Williams Memorial Library [mfilm No. 72] Item no. 1226. He has assigned it an ID number of B77429. Roud's text begins, "The merry time arriving,/To Smithfield how they're driving,/And everyone is striving/ To see the Lord Mayor's Coach" which does not agree with the text printed by Rimbault. Clearly there were *two* songs sharing the same title.

52. See Roy Palmer and Jon Raven, *The Rigs of the Fair* (Cambridge: Cambridge University Press, 1976), pp. 25–28.

Wit and Mirth and then again in Tom D'Urfey's *Pills to Purge Melancholy*, Vol. , p.169 (1719), "An Ancient Song of Bartholomew Fair" appeared. The date of 1700 is assigned in the *Roxburghe Ballads*, Vol. VII (London: The Ballad Society, 1890), p. 227 by editor J. Woodfall Ebsworth. An alternative reading in the sixth verse in *Pills to Purge Melancholy* in both the 1700 and 1719 editions reads:

> At every Door lies a hag, or a whore, and in *Hosier-Lane*, if I ain't mistaken;
> Zuch plenty there are of whores, you'll have a pair, To [sic, for] a single gammon of Bacon.

54. "Houses of boards" refers to the slapdash frame construction intended to be quickly knocked down at fair's end, then rebuilt in the next town.

55. The singer here is grousing about short-weighing.

56. "A Walk to Smithfield," printed for R. Hine, is in *Eighteenth Century Collections Online*, Gale Publications, Document number CW33079336706. A substantial portion, though edited for delicate ears, is printed in Morley, *Memoirs of Bartholomew Fair*, pp. 352–55.

57. A text is in Morley, pp. 249–250, which he acknowledges he has edited "in the name of cleanliness." Morley dates this to 1668; a copy in the Swem Library, William and Mary College, however, is dated 1705.

58. Morley, p. 397.

59. John Gay's ballad opera premiered at the Theatre Royal, in Lincoln's Inn Fields on January 29, 1728. It played for 63 days, a record run at the time. The music was based largely on traditional or, at least familiar, national airs borrowed, in the main, from Thomas D'Urfey's *Pills to Purge Melancholy*, William Thompson's *Orpheus Caledonius*, and Playford's *The Dancing Master*. The success of *The Beggar's Opera* prompted instant imitations, including *Hunter, or The Beggar's Wedding with Alterations. Consisting of English, Scots and Irish ballad tunes…*" and Charles Coffey's *The Devil to Pay* (1728) and *The Merry Cobbler* (1735). The alterations consisted of compressing the ballad opera if three acts, into one act, obviously eliminating many songs, and thereby making possible as many as six stressful performances each day. See Morley, p. 405, Willi Apfel's *Harvard Dictionary of Music* and Frederic Austin's liner notes to *The Beggar's Opera* (RCA Victor LM-6048).

60. Morley, p. 418.

61. Morley, p. 448–49.

62. "Mouthpieces" here are the fair's caterwauling barkers. The poem is printed in Morley, p. 452–53.

63. Morley, p. 453.

64. Morley, pp. 460–61.

65. www.lib.muohio.edu/multifacet/record/mu3ugb3158315

66. Morley, pp. 454–55.

67. Morley, p. 463.

68. Published with the long-s in 1799 by J. Davenport, No. 7, Little Catherine Street, Strand; and sold at No. 70 Turnmill Street, Clerkenwell in London. Microfilm/microform "18th Century, Reel 3022, No. 23; OL 16860191M. Roud has indexed "Bartholomew Fair, or The Humours of Smithfield," a Pitts broadside found in the Madden Collection (London Printers 2), a copy of which is on microfilm in the Vaughn-Williams mfilm No. 75, Item No. 84. Roud assigned it an ID number of B59630. Its first line also reads "O Bartelmy, Bartelmy Fair." The melody, under the title of "The Pyeman," does not appear in Simpson's *The British Broadside Ballad and Its Music*, nor in Keller's *Early American Songsters* compact disc.

69. See Theodore Edward Hook, *Killing No Murder, A Farce in Two Acts* Fifth edn. (London: Printed for C. Chapple, Pall-Mall, 1811), p. vi. In the "Advertisement," (p. viii), Hook praises Matthews, claiming "all my thanks are inadequate — but as I am unable to do justice to his professional talents, already so well known and appreciated, I may perhaps be allowed to say that all the approbation he receives in public as an actor, he fully deserves in private as a man." In that "advertisement," Hook rather cheekily praises the Methodist "Mr. Larpent for refusing his license, and creating an interest for the farce, I am chiefly obliged." See Hook, *Killing*, p. viii.

70. Hook, *Killing No Murder*, p. 3.

71. Hook, *Killing No Murder*, p. 5.

72. Hook, *Killing No Murder*, p. 43. For a brief history of the play's difficulties, see Frank Fowler and Frank Palmer, *Censorship in England*, (London: 1913; Frederick Blom, 1969.

73. Mr. Matthews' version is apparently first reprinted in the *Hibernian Cabinet: A Selection of the Most Popular Irish Songs, that have been lately written* (London Printed for T. Hughes, Ludgate Street, 1817), pp. 161–63.

74. Though greatly expanded (by Matthews himself?) this is still Roud ID number B41435.

75. Mathews freshened the cante-fable with new material, as in this printing from *The Melodist, and Mirthful Olio; An Elegant Collection of the Most Popular Songs, etc.* Vol. IV (London: Printed and Published by H. Arliss, Cheapside, 1829; and subsequently reprinted by Arliss the following year in *The Apollo*, Vol. II.

76. A. Hood wrote *Dickey Barrett: with his ancient mariners and much more ancient cannon!* in 1831, though it was not published until 1890 and subsequently reprinted by Southern Reprints, Aukland, N.Z., n.d.

77. www.mail-archive.com/lamoreaux-l@rootsweb.com/msg00243.html

78. See Henry DuBois Bailey, *Local Tales and Historical Sketches* (Fishkill Landing, NY: John W. Spaight, 1874).

79. cgriff@ccome.com

80. See www.thegalloper.com

81. Vance Randolph, *Ozark Folksongs*, Vol. III (Columbia, Mo: State Historical Society, 1949), p. 207, has "The Hamburger Fair." As a youth, the author's father sang the song with a different first line, "I went to the animal fair…"

82. Legman to Richard Reuss, dated 21st July 1975, courtesy of Judith Legman and Joanne Reuss. Legman added the full citation of *The Fountain of Mirth* as (Paisley, Scotland: G. Caldwell, 1840), pp. 19–23. Legman's copy is now in Ohio State University in Columbus. The text here is reprinted from *The Fountain of Mirth* by John Ashton's *Modern Street Ballads* (London: Chatto and Windus, 1888), pp. 110–115.

83. "Padolo" does not seem to be in the *Shorter OED* or standard slang dictionaries of the 19th Century.

84. Randolph, in Vol III of *Ozark Folksongs*, p. 206, carried notice of the advertisement.

85. Morley, p. 493.

86. *The Spirit of the Times* for Saturday, March 19, 1859, p. 42, placed the show in rural Mississippi, as noted in Arthur P. Hudson, *Humor of the Old Deep South* (New York: The MacMillan Co., 1936), pp. 272–74.

87. "Bob Hart's Plantation Songster" (New York: Dick and Fitzgerald, Publishers, 18 Ann Street; sur-stamped "For All Goods advertised in this book, address Wehman Bros., 146 Park Row, New York, pp. 63–64. Norm Cohen, *A Finding List of American Secular Songsters* (Murfressboro: Middle Tennessee State University, 2002), pp. 32, dates this to 1862. That this is included in a "Plantation" songster suggests that the original sheet music was intended for a blackface minstrel show.

88. *Yale Literary Quarterly*, Vol. 27, p. 296, (1862).

89. The date, obviously incorrect, was assigned by the Levy Collection, Johns Hopkins Collection.

90. This is an aurally learned version with an approximate, arbitrary date of 1930 courtesy of David Ruch (text) and Jane Keefer (tune).

91. "Selected Songs" was privately printed by William Allen Hayes (Cambridge: Press of John Wilson and Sons, 1866), pp. 46–48.

92. Jonathan Lighter, editor of the *The Historical Dictionary of America Slang*, to be concluded by Oxford University Press, has defined "over the left" as a negative, approximately equivalent to the contemporary "like hell."

93. *Carmina Yalensia: A Complete and Accurate Collection of Yale College Songs with Piano Accompaniment Compiled and Arranged by Ferd. V.D. Garretson* (New York: Taintor Brothers, 1867). Sigmund Spaeth, *Read 'Em and Weep: The Songs You Forgot to Remember* (New York: Halcyon House, 1939), pp. 75–77, has an identical text, entitled "Menagerie." Other college versions are to be found in *Carmina Princetonia: The University Song Book*, 9th edn (Newark, N.J.: Martin R. Dennis, 1898); *The Most Popular*

College Songs (New York: Himes, Noble and Eldredge, c.1904) and *The Remick Favorite Collection of College Songs* (New York and Detroit: Jerome H. Remick Co, c. 1909).

94. Steve Gardham, who sent the author a copy of the original printing of the song, has credited Lee (d. 1906) with the music and the otherwise unknown Frank W. Green with the music. Gardham's original email was dated September 27, 2003. "One of Leybourn's obituary writers suggested, "Fully sixty percent of the successful comic songs played and whistled and barrel-organed about the world for the past twenty years have been composed by him [Lee]." Cited in Paul Watt, "Catalogue of Stardust Melodies, An Exhibition of Sheet Music from the Rare Books Collection," 22 June–5 September 2011, Monash University.

95. This version appeared in *The Beauty of the Blondes'* [sic] *Songster* (New York: Robert M. De Witt) pp.112–113. Norm Cohen's *American Secular Songsters*, p. 43, dates its publication to approximately 1870. Identical reprints appeared in *The Old Clown's 'W-H-O-A January' Songster, Yankee Robinson's'* [sic] *Beautiful Amazon Songster*, all published by Robert De Witt. (Cohen dates all three from 1870 although the *Yankee Robinson Songster* clearly reads 1876. The Lee song, without credit, is reprinted in *The Clown's 'Shoo Fly' Songster* dated 1870 and reprinted in Marcello Truzzi, "Folksongs of the American Circus," *New York Folklore Quarterly*, XXIV (September, 1968), pp. 170–71. Cohen dates the songster to 1870 in a De Witt printing. *The American College Songster*, compiled by Samuel Chester Andrews (Ann Arbor, Michigan: Sheehan and Co., 1876), pp. 185–86, reprints the text, but not the music; it contains only minor errata.

96. *Carmina Collegensia: A Complete Collection of the Songs of the American Colleges*, edited by Henry Randall Waite, rev edn. (Boston: Oliver Ditson, c. 1876). The McGill University Songbook of 1921 has an identical text. The McGill text also corrects the menagerie's owner to Van Amburgh. Under the title of "Van Amburg Is the Man," "Chip" Sandresky forwarded a text and tune to John Patrick prior to September 27, 2003. Sandresky noted the disparity of text and tune his mother sang to both him and his siblings, and "continues to sing to her grandchildren." Thus a popular song of the 1860's persists in oral tradition as a lullaby. As an aside, he added, "I enjoyed the 'Wild West Show.' It reminds me of some drinking songs from my fraternity days."

97. Alfred P. Burbank, the editor of *A Collection of Humorous, Dramatic and Dialect Selections* (New York: Dick and Fitzgerald, Publishers, 1878), pp. 44–46, provides the first report of the "raree song" tradition.

98. William C. Smith, *Queen City Yesterdays: Sketches of Cincinnati in the Eighties* (Crawfordsville, Indiana: R.E. Banta 1902[?].)

99. "James S. Burdette's Irishman's Panorama" in *Wit and Humor of the Age... with The Philosophy of Wit and Humor by Melville D. Landon, A.M.* (Lexington, Kentucky: Huffman & Johnson, 1884), pp. 489–90.

100. Smith, *Queen City Yesterdays*, p. 41.

101. "Michael Casey Exhibiting His Panorama" is from a compact disc entitled "Actionable Offenses: Indecent Phonograph Recordings from the 1890s" (Champaign,

Illinois: Archeophone Records, 2007) No. 1007. It is performed by Willy Smith; the text is attributed to James White.

102. "The Aurora," Vol. XV, Senior Class Annual, Michigan State Normal College, Yipsilanti, Michigan, 1908) p. 206.

103. "Spring and Summer School Celebrations," edited by Alice M. Kellogg (Philadelphia: The Penn Publishing Company, 1913), pp. 181 ff.

104. John Brophy and Eric Partridge, *The Long Trail* (New York: London House and Maxwell, 1965) pp. 230–31. The same is in *The Daily Telegraph Dictionary of Tommies' Songs and Slang* (Barnsley, South Yorkshire: Frontline Books, 2008).

105. This description was offered by R.S. Breakey, University of Michigan, ca. 1918, collected by Marcia Guilbert, East Lansing, Michigan, May, 1956.

106. "The Cruise of the New Decameron" (Privately issued for C. Nile Dix and his Friends. Boston, n.p. 1920) in a mimeographed 52-page, single spaced typescript. The name is obviously a pseudonym: Senile Dicks. The song appears on p. 48. A copy is in the Institute for Sex Research, Bloomington, Indiana.

107. "Capt. Billy's Whiz Bang,' Winter Annual, 1921–22 Vol. III, No. 26 (October 5, 1921) (Robbinsdale, Minnesota: W.K. Fosett [spelling?]).

108. *McGill University Songbook*, vol.1 (McGill University Students' Council, 1921), pp. 79–83; 104–106, contains "Menagerie," with 14 stanzas *and* "Hamburgh" with nine stanzas.

109. Jonathan Lightner by email to Ballad-L@listserve.Indiana.edu, December 1, 2006, noted: "In the June, 1925, issue of *The American Mercury*, gadfly critic H.L. Mencken interrupted his review of James Stevens' Paul Bunyan book to dilate upon some failings of the "folk-lorists of the Republic." Lightner added, "The version that Mencken knew was of the 'Larry, Turn the Crank' variety printed as 'The Hamburg Show' two years later in *Immortalia*, pp. 153–54. An indication of just how widespread the recitation may have been by 1930 is that precisely *none* of the creatures Mencken enumerates appear in the *Immortalia* text of 1927."

110. *Immortalia: An Anthology of American Ballads, Sailors' Songs, Cowboy Songs... For the First Time Brought Together in Book Form in 1927 by a Gentleman about Town*, rep. edn (Long Beach, California: Immortalia Press, 1975).

111. O. U. Schweinickle, *The Book of a Thousand Laughs* (n.p.n.d) may be found at:
www.horntip.com/html/books_&_MSS/1920s/1928_the_book_of_a_thousand_laughs_%28PB%29/index.htm

112. www.horntip.com/html/books_&_MSS/1920s/1928ca_a_collection_of_sea_songs_and_ditties__dave_e_jones_%28HC%29/index.htm

113. "Bibliotheque Erotique, Vol. 2" (Ostensibly published by The Society for Sociological and Psychological Research in Literature, London, 1929); in reality, published by "Mac" (which Richard Reuss has described as a "fly-by-night outfit, probably in Detroit, 1929"), pp. 506–14.

114. William Joyce Cowen, *They Gave Him a Gun* (NY: Grosset & Dunlap, 1936), has a fragmentary verse or two, expurgated [?] and non-bawdy. "Hun" dates this to World War I.

115. Martin Page includes in his *For Gawdsake Don't Take Me* (London: Hart-Davis, MacGibbon, 1976), pp. 124–25. In an email to Cray, September 24, 2003, Steve Gardham pointed out that the Green-Lee "Royal Wild Beast Show" also contains a verse about the oozley bird.

116. Collected by Shirley Swaney, then of Grand Rapids, Michigan. This too is from the Reuss files.

117. Contributed to the Richard Reuss files by Nancy T. Hunter of East Lansing, Michigan, who heard it at Swarthmore, Pennsylvania, in 1944.

118. "There are many more verses, but my informant (Sally Boone of East Lansing, Michigan on November 3, 1955) could not recall them. She said she heard the song this summer when she worked at a resort in New York State," wrote Ms. Pat Roberts, of Kalamazoo, Michigan, on her contribution to the Reuss files.

119. Courtesy of Simon Furey in an email to Cray, July 3, 2011.

120. Courtesy of Ewan McVicar in an email to Cray on July 3, 2011.

121. Email to Cray from John Roberts, who learned these verses in the UK.

122. In contributing to the Reuss files, Ms. Sue Schrader of South Bend, Indiana, noted, "My informant, Judy Vincent of Indiana University on July 28, 1962, learned this song from college students from 'Old Miss' [University of Mississippi] in the summer of 1961.

123. This version was collected in Los Angeles by Suzanne Bray on October 14, 1967. The informant, BR, learned the song at a UCLA fraternity. "He knew many more verses." These, he told Bray, were some of the newer ones. The text, deposited in UCLA's Archive of California and Western Folklore was in a file amassed by Richard Reuss.

124. The unpublished manuscript of Kenneth S. Goldstein and Edith Fowke, "Bawdy Ballads and Dirty Ditties from Ontario and Newfoundland" has a text contributed by Woody Lambe and recorded by Ms. Fowke in 1963. Lambe's version contained these unusual verses. See too Ms. Fowke's article, "A Sampling of Bawdy Ballads and Dirty Ditties from Ontario," in Bruce Jackson, ed. *Folklore and Society: Essays in Honor of Benjamin A. Botkin* (Hatboro, Pennsylvania: Folklore Associates, Inc., 1966), pp. 45–62.

125. Simon Furey in an email to Cray, July 3, 2011.

126. Walsh added this note: "For whatever it is worth, here's where I picked these up; most of them turn up at all the rugby parties and are common properties, but a few can be pinned down more closely. (Stanza five was from a Notre Dame player, as were eight and nine. Six was from a New Zealander going to Palmer Chiropractic College in Davenport, Iowa.)

127. From Kenneth Burke, *Language as Symbolic Action* (Berkeley: University of California Press, 1966), p. 325. Courtesy of John Lighter.

128. Jerome Epstein in an email to Cray, July 3, 2011, who added, "There must be hundreds of verses."

129. Community standards evolve and the shock value wanes. A generation after Anaya, *The New Yorker* magazine routinely prints declensions of the word "fuck." An evening of new plays at the theatre will produce one or more such words — without an audience's murmur. Meanwhile, at another level, hashers, that is "drinkers with a running problem," race cross-country distances over a pre-marked course to end up in a drinking session of stupendous consumption, song and mixed company camaraderie. Their repertoire includes "The Wild West Show."

130. Stephen Anaya's contributions are in the Reuss files at UCLA.

131. Courtesy of the late Charles Baumerich and Paul Woodford.

132. A "balls-up" is the Anzac-Canadian-British equivalent of a "fuck up."

133. [Harry Morgan?], *More Rugby Songs* (London: Sphere Books Limited, 1968), pp.101–103. The book was copyrighted by Morgan, the presumed compiler.

134. The Melbourne, Australia, YWCA has a triangular sign.

135. These versions were from United States Air Force currency, collected by C.W. Getz and published in Getz's *The Wild Blue Yonder*, Vol. II (Burlingame, California: The Redwood Press, 1968), pp. HH2–HH3. The songs are arbitrarily assigned to their date of publication. A similar text — one with three added verses found in other versions/variants of the cante-fable — is to be found in the songbook of the 335th Fighter Squadron "Chiefs," then active in the first Iraqi war, ca. 1991.

136. From the Reuss files, this was collected by Peter Thomas and Gary Waghorn from a Windsor, Ontario, national guard regiment in December, 1970.

137. Entitled "National Engineering Book of Song and Verse," with no publisher other source of source of publication, this *may* have been originally put together as "The Engineers' Handbook" by the Engineering Fraternity, University of Newcastle, New South Wales.

138. From the Reuss files, as collected by Jack Frisch, May 17, 1971, from FW, who played for the Windsor Borderers Rugby Club. FW had learned it in British Columbia in the late 1960's when he played college rugby.

139. Courtesy of Jonathan Lighter.

140. This was collected by John Sherry from the Indiana University Rugby Club in the fall of 1976.

141. This citation and text are through the courtesy of J.B. Hanon. Edwards' field notes stated, "This is neither a song nor a recitation, but an example, of a nonsense piece a form of entertainment once popular around the campfire and at front-parlour get-togethers (though this particular one is not really front parlour fare)."

141. Courtesy of Jonathan Lighter.

142. Reuss files, courtesy of Joanne Reuss.

143. This citation and text are through the courtesy of J.B. Hanon. Edwards' field notes stated, "This is neither a song nor a recitation, but an example, of a nonsense piece a form of entertainment once popular around the campfire and at front-parlour get-togethers (though this particular one is not really front parlour fare)."

144. Extracted from *The Official Book of Bawdy Ballads* (Camberwell, London: Futura Publications, Ltd., 1979) pp. 172–74.

145. This version was posted on Jack Horntip's website (horntip.com.html/books¬_&_Mss). It was taken from the mimeographed "The Unexpurgated Roadtrip Songbooks" which Horntip dates to ca. 1982. Horntip's source commented, "I really only recall 'the punch line' as sung by my late friend Scott Welch in the early 80's. Hardly PC [politically correct]. The Monback and Motee tribes were attempting to say 'come on back' and 'hold the door.'"

146. All are euphemisms for sex organs.

147. Email from Ronnie Clark to Cray, July 2, 2011.

148. Gary R. Smith and Alan Maki, *Death in the Delta* (New York: Ballantine, 1995), p. 28. Courtesy of Jonathan Lighter.

149. See mudcat.org/thread.cfm?threadid=76352.

150. This partial text of "The Wild West Show" is from the 1985 versions of the 43rd Tactical Squadron's songbook compiled by Paul Woodford and the late Charles "Zippy" Baumerich. See pwoodford.net.hashblog/

CPSIA information can be obtained
at www.ICGtesting.com
Printed in the USA
FFOW01n2201071116
29059FF